African American Folk Healing

Stephanie Y. Mitchem

African American Folk Healing

New York University Press • *New York and London*

NEW YORK UNIVERSITY PRESS
New York and London
www.nyupress.org

Library of Congress Cataloging-in-Publication Data
Mitchem, Stephanie Y., 1950–
African American folk healing / Stephanie Mitchem.
p.   cm.
Includes bibliographical references and index.
ISBN-13: 978-0-8147-5731-4 (cloth : alk. paper)
ISBN-10: 0-8147-5731-6 (cloth : alk. paper)
ISBN-13: 978-0-8147-5732-1 (pbk : alk. paper)
ISBN-10: 0-8147-5732-4 (pbk : alk. paper)
1. African-Americans—Folklore. 2. African-Americans—Medicine.
I. Title.
GR111.A47M575 2007
398.2089'96073—dc22   2007001899

New York University Press books are printed on acid-free paper,
and their binding materials are chosen for strength and durability.

Manufactured in the United States of America
c 10 9 8 7 6 5 4 3 2 1
p 10 9 8 7 6 5 4 3 2 1

This book is dedicated to Cassie, Spain, Jordan, Anderson, and Emma
—and to Cousin Vell, who has led the way in healing our family's past.

—Ashé

Contents

Acknowledgments

This book would not have happened without the input and direction of many people. The women and men I interviewed are the first ones I want to thank because their comments changed the shape of the book; because of them, I learned to look at the African American folk healing with new eyes. I, alone, did not find all the people I interviewed. David Daniels, Rosalind Hinton, and Brenda Miller introduced me to healers across the country and made the scope of the book possible.

Janet Langlois, at Wayne State University in Detroit, facilitated locating the Folk Archives, which are an important source for this book. Margaret Raucher and the staff in the Walter P. Reuther Library of Labor and Urban Affairs at Wayne State made my time in the Folk Archives easier because of their assistance, even with cranky tape recorders.

A research fund award from the University of Detroit Mercy College of Liberal Arts and Education provided some needed financial assistance to complete my research.

Conversations with others helped me refine the writing, particularly Linda Barnes and Ann Eskridge who listened and advised along the way. Jennifer Hammer, with patience and support, provided editorial wisdom that I sorely needed.

I am grateful to each of these who shared stories and expertise and resources. Thank you.

Introduction

When I was a child, a nosebleed was treated by holding a silver quarter on the back of the neck. Earaches were treated with sweet oil drops. A child with mumps was rubbed on the neck with sardine oil. Measles called for a bath in chamomile. Various teas were given to children and senior adults at the beginning of spring or winter to build the blood or to eliminate worms. Castor oil and Vicks; glycerin and sassafras tea; paregoric and rock candy; whiskey and Three Sixes, all were part of our home health care routine. At the same time, my mother's mother had been a practical nurse, and we melded aspirin and rubbing alcohol into our own range of folk practices. Doctors' visits were but one tool for self-care, and not always the first line of defense. These kinds of practices continue in my family and did not disappear as older members died.

While visiting my adult daughter, I mentioned that I was going to get my hair trimmed. She immediately began to caution me about how the hair was discarded or handled. I was surprised: when had I communicated these ideas to her? I remember that my mother had often told me to take such care. *Her* grandmother had said that if hair were thrown out, birds would pick it up and make nests with it—resulting in headaches. How did my child, living in the twenty-first century, come to adopt such ideas?

I think often of these family groundings as I study and research black folk healing. Folk healing ideas, stories, and practices are common in black communities, and are often communicated through the women, reaching across regions where African Americans reside. We carry these folk remedies across generations. We find ways to continue practices in countryside and cityscape. They are not simply healing practices; they are linked to expressions of faith because they delineate aspects of a holistic epistemology. The belief that birds take cut hair and we get headaches as a result does not deny the existence of a Supreme Being but emphasizes the wonders of the Divine in new ways.

The stories and folk sayings that inform the concepts of folk healing are methods of defining our existence, often in sharp contrast to what is being said about black people among the majority of Americans. This book explores and contextualizes black American cultural concepts within folk healing traditions; its importance is that it opens new dialogical possibilities among all Americans. The stories about black folk healing are about American life and, sometimes, about our shared meanings or common misconceptions.

Researching and writing this book is tied to my passion for understanding what underlies black faith expressions. If we can speak of "foundations of theology" that rest beneath the epistemological foundations of Western religious thought, then we can certainly find the roots of black faith understandings. This book's exploration into the theme of healing is but one route.

Much of my research has been on African American women's faith lives, yet their religiosity is never separate from the black communities in which they stand. When applied to African Americans, the word *spirituality* is often a substitute for theological foundations. The theological foundations of black religiosity are shrouded in misunderstandings. Part of the reason is that so much of black life has been understood in a mythologized framework of interpretations of white researchers, who applied their own meanings to black folks' actions. For example, a white colleague and I were speaking about research on African Americans and cancer. The colleague was developing an outcome-based program that might affect African Americans' cancer testing rates. The program would determine its success on the number of black people tested for different forms of cancer. I replied that my interests focused on black Americans' concepts of health, illness, and healing in light of spirituality in order to better understand health practices. I then presented several examples of the approaches that black people take regarding health care, resulting in what I called self-directed healing methods. "Ah," the researcher replied. "I often wondered why so many black people were fatalistic when diagnosed with cancer." I understood intellectually how the researcher reached this interpretation of black behavior: many African Americans approach illness and health from a cultural framework that does not match the expectations of those in medical professions. The responses of black people to illness seems, to some, odd or even dangerous. But emotionally, I heard the word *fatalistic* as affirmation of racist assumptions about black concepts in healing practices. With this hearing, the word implies that African Americans do not have their own culturally centered responses in place when faced with potentially terminal illness. The word suggested resignation rather than resistance in explaining practices in black American contexts that fit but may not translate to Western frameworks.

This book on African American folk healing explores precisely these non-Western-sanctioned practices. It looks into the culturally derived concepts that black people have about wellness, and how the concepts have evolved, persisted in their relevance, and continued to offer remedies to heal black minds, bodies, and communities. This has not been easy to accomplish because the multiple facets of African American folk healing elude simplistic categorization. Therefore, folklore, religion, history, culture studies, and ethnography each add necessary components to the construction of this study.

The definition of African American folk healing that is the basis for discussions throughout this book is as follows:

> African American folk healing is the creatively developed range of activities and ideas that aim to balance and renew life. Although multiple cultures' healing and spirituality traditions may be utilized, an epistemological frame of reference is embedded in the craft that reflects African American cultural perspectives. In this view, human life is understood relationally as part of the interconnected, shared web of the universe. Sickness, then, is derived not only from germs but also from situations that break relational connections. The born, unborn, and dead are all intertwined, particularly through familial connections.
>
> Consequently, death is not a final break with life because the spirit/ soul continues and may be able to interact from the next plane of existence. Story and action are intertwined in the performance of healing: the story tells of relationships and then action must follow. Within this scheme, the person of the healer, rootworker, or conjurer is important. This individual learns to orchestrate or "fix" the natural, spiritual, and relational aspects of life. However, all healing is not limited to professional healers: those who know which herbs, roots, or elements to use for certain effects can access healing when needed.

In this book, we will view folk healing with the widest possible lens, interpreting actions and events beyond the levels at which they are normally considered. Understanding African American folk healing is more than simply identifying herbologists and their wisdom about plant life. African American folk healing can be found embedded in black religious life, art, social activism, and marital relationships.

Folk healing exists in many forms beyond kitchen cupboards in black American communities. The home stands as the first educational center that shapes awareness of both personal care and concepts of healing. Religious meanings are passed on in these early teachings, connecting healing with spirituality and defining health with a state of spiritual well-being. From this home grounding, African Americans learn to apply healing concepts in more diffuse ways: within the community, in encounters with others, and in translating concepts from the media and medical institutions. Folk healing operates in black communities as both individual and communal practice, with attitudes ranging from revulsion to reverence.

The basic definition provided above needs a bit more fleshing out before we move on. It is practical to think of African American folk healing as a crossroads at which several concepts and material realities converge and very different views emerge. As a cultural grounding, folk healing serves to interpret and interact with wider American society. In this way, folk healing is a form of folklore, and language is given a central role. Conceptually, African American folk healing encompasses black identities, cultures, and spiritualities. Yet African American folk healing does not have a set of simple principles to which all adhere; rather, it attests the diversity among black Americans. However, similarities are found across regions in the epistemology.

Developing from its historical roots, African American folk healing continues today in several forms. Folk healing, for example, is reflected in attempts to "heal" the effects of enslavement. Black folk healing is discernable in some dimensions of faith healing, and the folk concepts of healing flow easily into much social activist work undertaken by African Americans.

The relationships between black American cultural production and white American societies can be seen in the historical development and understanding of black folk healing. The Slave Narratives quoted in chapter 1 will present one view of raced relations; these accounts contrast with those presented from the Folk Archives in chapter 3. Both of these show differences in the race relations that are shown in chapter 7. Folk healing is a crossroads that offers a glimpse into the ways that culture hybridizes within black communities in relationship to the wider American cultural framework, such as historic interactions with Native Americans or the contemporary use of the Internet.

Folk healing continues to have meaning and value in black communities, but there are many questions to answer. For example: What are the healing activities and ideas of African American folk healing that aim to balance and renew life? How and why have historical instances of these healing practices carried over into the present? What are the relationships between physical and spiritual healing? How has urban living impacted African Americans' understandings of folk healing? How have remnants of folk healing changed in light of greater access to information from the formalized medical profession?

African American folk healing is often narrowly presented as a kind of post–Jim Crow hangover, with the implication that as soon as black people are fully acculturated into American society, they will no longer need such magical thinking. For some, African American folk healing is evidence of a continued "primitivism" among black people. I argue differently: African American folk healing continues because of cultural conceptualizations that give life to black communities, including the economic and spiritual needs that these practices address. To demonstrate how African American folk healing has persisted and developed, I will primarily focus on the twentieth into the twenty-first centuries. The practices and ideas in the broad spectrum I include under African American folk healing represent one of many often unacknowledged but significant discourses between black and mainstream America. *African American Folk Healing* will provide an important interpretive framework for understanding multiple dimensions of this aspect of ongoing and developing black cultural expressions.

The book has two parts. The first provides background and history, setting out key concepts and ideas. To this end, chapter 1 expands the working definition of African American folk healing, offering greater detail. In addition to exploring the importance of language and the concept of the "folk," I draw from interviews of the Federal Writers' Project (1936–1939). Chapter 2 considers African American concepts of healing in contrast to the ways that black bodies are conceptualized. Because healing is itself a concept that is connected with medicine, this chapter will contrast black folk traditions with institutionalized biomedicine.

Chapter 3 makes the case for the continuations of black folk healing from the twentieth into the twenty-first century. The ways that folk practices traveled with black migrants from the South to the North of the United States present one lens through which to view adaptations of black cultural patterns. I am indebted to the Wayne State University folklore collection, which contains 1970s interviews of African Americans who had migrated from the South to Detroit earlier in the century in search of work. This collection was instrumental in illuminating twentieth-century developments of African American folk healing.

The first three chapters inform the second part of the book, which explores various forms of the twenty-first century presence of African American folk healing. Chapter 4 draws on two interviews with healers. The ways they blend past thinking with modern practices demonstrate how African American folk healing is renewed through processes of hybridity. This chapter also locates African American folk healing more concretely in what I term a black mystical tradition. The next two chapters look at dimensions of folk healing as culturally based ideas that are applied to daily life. Chapter 5 considers the healing of black identities through methods such as naming and reparations, among others. In light of this healing activity, I discuss the idea of folk healing within a black intellectual tradition. Chapter 6 considers how spirituality and religion are related to black folk healing. The last chapter, chapter 7, focuses on the commercial expressions of African American folk healing by examining some modern sources of information, from candle shops to the Internet to a hoodoo class. These contemporary practices express a black spirituality of healing that, because of its importance, I also consider in this chapter how African Americans interact with death in light of folk healing.

Through these chapters, I present my arguments that black folk healing is included in African American intellectual and mystical traditions. The intellectual aspect of folk healing expresses an ethical perspective, based on values, that can inform the individual or the community. Stated another way, the content of folk healing, even as it changes over time, is based on cultural reasoning, not chance. Simultaneously, a specific spirituality is in operation that defines a holistic cosmology and these are components of a black mystical tradition.

Black Americans have often been thought of in a too-constricting framework. Analysis of African American folk healing, particularly in light of intellectual and mystical traditions, challenges boundaries that have been created in past scholarship or in the American popular imagination.

The joy of writing this book has been the opportunity to explore the depth of black American wisdom. As I talked about the book with other African Americans, I came to appreciate how intimate these healing concepts have been to black communal life experiences. Folk healing develops creative constructions that spring from culturally based wisdom. Such constructions work to resist dehumanization while simultaneously building upon the spiritual dimensions of an epistemological framework. Hence, in our conversations, we often struggled to find the right words to express the ideas that are embedded in our lives. Falling into the complexities this study uncovered was unintentional. Yet, at the end of the day, only a multilayered portrait of this facet of a people's cultural expression will get to the roots of ideas and practices known as African American folk healing.

PART I

Historical Paths to Healing

1

Stories and Cures

Defining African American Folk Healing

I've heard if a turkledove, when the season first starts, comes to your house and starts moanin', it's a sign you is goin' to move out and somebody else id goin' to move in.

If a squinch owl starts howlin' 'round your house, and you turn your shoe upside down at the door, they sure will hush. Now I know that's so. . . . And I've heard the old folks say if you start any place and have to go back, make a circle on the ground and spit in it or you'll have bad luck.

—Clark Hill, Pine Bluff, Arkansas, in the WPA
Slave Narratives Project, Arkansas Narratives,
Volume 2, Part 3, Federal Writers' Project,
1936–1939[1]

Tracing Black Folk Healing

African American folk healing may be defined as the creatively developed range of activities and ideas that aim to balance and renew life. To explore African American folk healing is to open up a vista of black American concepts about life, bodies, death, and nature. Such concepts may have spiritual referents, may move into political action, or may serve as the homegrown analysis of society. To create and maintain such ideas, structured from African cultural orientations, American pragmatism, and information from other cultures, attests the savvy of African Americans as a people. Yet, tracing folk healing in black communities or through history to uncover its meanings is not a simple task. Discerning these meanings also entails tangling with layers of racism and centuries of separatism that created limited, unreal images of black Americans.

Enslavement legally ended in the former slave states with President Lincoln's Emancipation Proclamation in 1863. Yet, African Americans continued to live in separate, segregated, and oppressive conditions. What might have happened had the promise of equality been fulfilled during Reconstruction (roughly 1863–1880) is only a matter of speculation. What did happen in fact was another form of capture and control of black Americans. The Supreme Court ruling in the *Plessy v. Ferguson* case in 1896 held that the Constitution could not eliminate the perceived hierarchy of races, with its superior-white and inferior-black belief systems and, therefore, separate but equal was constitutional. Separation of races became the norm; a genuine awareness of the depth and richness of black lives was underrated. Attempts to analyze the complex layers of black life were limited and often ran counter to the mainstream of white American scholarship.

Despite these limitations, one source in particular holds valuable information about African American folk healing practices of the past. The United States government established the Works Progress Administration in 1935 to provide employment to some Americans in various fields during the Great Depression. The Federal Writers' Project, started in 1936, was part of this larger effort. The project gathered oral accounts of black Americans. The accounts of twenty-three hundred black men and women were gathered throughout the South between 1936 and 1938. Some of these interviews specifically focused on narratives of enslavement.

Because of strict segregation laws in effect in the 1930s throughout the South, mostly white researchers collected these accounts. One notable exception is anthropologist and novelist Zora Neale Hurston, who was hired by the project but whose white regional editor rejected portions of her work. In recent years, these documents have been published.[2] Hurston's intent was to capture the daily lives of workers in Florida, not to collect slave narratives. However, the treatment accorded of her work signals a larger issue: it has historically been within the power of white, middle-class, Protestant communities to generate the generally accepted images of black Americans. As a result, woven into the folk talk around black healing practices are questions of authority and validity and race. Themes of authority, creation of images, language, and interaction between African Americans and other communities are threads running throughout this book, just as they run through the dynamics of the relationships themselves. As we aim for a more accurate picture, our tracing of black folk healing needs to begin with the words of black Americans. The Slave Narratives, one portion of the Federal Writers' Project, provide access to excellent first-person narratives. These narratives are a starting line for a closer look at the dynamics of folk healing. Yet, the meanings of the speakers themselves are often obscured; the meanings need to be teased from the texts. Reflecting the time period (1930s) in which the data were collected, information is often presented without contexts, lending itself to the interpretation of the reader. Most of the researchers heavily use the Negro dialect to give a sense of the information's being "authentically black." Words such as " 'fore," " 'bout," " 'em," "chillun," "warn't," and "wuss" appear throughout the sections. Some of the words are creatively spelled, further conveying a sense commonly held by white people during that time of ignorant black people. As Hurston's experiences with the project indicate, the white regional editors may have added one more level of interpretation in the ways they excluded or revised the interviews. Despite these problems of language, contexts, editing, and selection of material, the Slave Narratives, and the Federal Writers' Project remain notable sources of historical information about black cultural realities.

The interviews related to folk healing provide essential information relevant to African American practices and beliefs during enslavement and the early twentieth century. From curing a backache to smallpox, a variety of homegrown medical remedies utilized the elements at hand, such as black pepper, roots, and stones. Some of the cures were pragmatic, such as how to prevent a fall while crossing a creek (hold a small stick crosswise between the teeth). Yet, there are problems built into the selections. The very listing of these cures, because they are given without context, reinforces public images of black people as ignorant and perhaps childlike. The listings of cures without contexts also suggest to the popular imagination that folk healing is related to only plants and practices. The exception to this approach is the work of folklorists who place healing in a larger scheme that links the practices of healers to language and performance. These ideas are discussed in more detail later in this chapter.

The Slave Narratives contain another text that is barely below the surface. Although the racist mores of society structured how white and black Americans were supposed to interact in general, these mores were strictly defined in matters of research as well: black people were consistently identified as primitive objects that must be interpreted by the white researchers. The point of view was most often that of white America, which was further derogatory of black people. The socialized understandings are important to note here because significant changes in these relationships occurred during the twentieth century, as will be seen in later chapters. A very brief look at one of the Slave Narratives' researchers in the 1930s brings some of these issues to the fore.

Georgia was an especially hardened center of racist activity: in Atlanta, in September 1906, a race riot eventuated in the lynching of twenty-five black people and the wounding of another hundred. White men were in a killing rage because of alleged rapes of white women by black men. White racists throughout the country continued to level all kinds of hostility against black Americans; race riots and lynchings became commonplace.

The national climate brought distinction to Louise Oliphant, one of the white researchers in Georgia in the 1930s. Of her six accounts included in the Library of Congress's WPA archives, some defined the "Work, Play, Food, Clothing, Marriage, etc."[3] of the former slaves that she interviewed. These accounts provide some contextualization to her documentation of folk healing. For instance, she introduced the collection on the mistreatment of slaves: "Mistreatment at the hands of their masters and the watchdog overseers is outstanding in the memory of most of them." After one brief interview about the "good white folk," in spite of the racist times, Oliphant turned her respondent to several painful recollections of the horrors of enslavement: "Bob Lampkin was the meanest slave owner I ever knowed. He would beat his slaves and everybody else's he caught in the road."[4] Thus, Oliphant demonstrated compassion for her interviewees. Moreover, she was able to get some of the testimonies past the Slave Narratives' regional editor.

Oliphant's approach was in sharp contrast to that of other researchers from Georgia at that time, some of whom defended slavery as an institution that made the former slaves happy with their state. For example, an interviewer interpreted the words of a former slave, called "Aunt Adeline": "She told about the slaves living in the Quarters—log houses all in a long row near the 'white folks' house,' and how happy they were. 'My Marster had lots of niggers.'"[5] As a reflection of that time's reality, Oliphant's compassion and sympathy were the best one could hope for in the public demonstrations of race relations in Georgia in the 1930s.

Turning to Oliphant's accounts related directly to folk healing, one is entitled "Conjuration"[6] and another is "Folk Remedies and Superstitions."[7] The titles indicate two points for consideration. The first point is the confusing range of names given to aspects of African American folk healing: *conjure, conjuration, superstition, hoodoo,* and *juju.* In particular, *hoodoo, conjure,* and sometimes *faith healing* are very often perceived as the entirety of African American folk healing. Yet there exists a wide range of practices and views beyond these that attests to wider statements of African American creativity. As a definition to use here, *hoodoo* (or *conjure*) is a set of practices and beliefs that draw on nature and its perceived energies in order to shape preferred conditions.

However, *hoodoo* is also dropped into negative categories, particularly magic, witchcraft, or sorcery. A traditional Protestant Christian concept views magic as breaking with the natural, God-created order of life to align with evil forces, such as the devil, for malevolent purposes. These images fill Western literature and art, and history books include accounts of witch burnings. Even as some popular television shows or books over the past twenty-five years have shown happy, well-intentioned, good witches, the potential for evil enchantment or deceptive illusions is ever present. Participation in magic is, in that traditional Western Christian mindset, the equivalent of accepting damnation. In an African American epistemology, on the other hand, the supernatural is not automatically to be feared but to be respected. The charms and spells of hoodoo may bring power to the user. Belief in this power indicates some dimensions of the basic definition of African American folk healing: that human life is understood relationally; it is part of the interconnected shared web of the universe; human life and death are contiguous realms connected by spirit; and the conjurer knows how to influence each of these dimensions.

This leads to the second point derived from the titles of Oliphant's folklore accounts. Discussions of the supernatural will be different from black and white Americans' perspectives. This was especially true in Georgia in the 1930s: Oliphant may have believed exactly as the people she interviewed but could never publicly declare it. A public discussion of magic, witchcraft, or spells from a black epistemological perspective would have been barely possible during those years.

There was a shift in this attitude over the twentieth century, as demonstrated by the sharp contrast in the twenty-first-century attitudes expressed in chapter 7.

Under "Remedies and Superstitions," Oliphant gathered assorted information that referred to healing ways. She did not cite extended interviews but developed lists of various cures. "Tea made from rue is good for stomach worms. Corn shuck tea is good for measles; fodder tea for asthma. Goldenrod tea is good for chills and fever."[8] Oliphant does not indicate how the belief was learned, if it had links to other racial or ethnic groups, or if it was widely held. The list does indicate the use of plant life that was readily available in farming communities.

Oliphant turned her attention toward the folklore that encompasses specific cures, perhaps recognizing that healing for her respondents went beyond curative herbs. For instance, she listed some dream interpretations as part of healing: "To dream of blood is a sign of trouble. To dream of fish is a sign of motherhood. To dream of eggs is a sign of trouble unless the eggs are broken. If the eggs are broken, your trouble is ended."[9] Relationships could be read or corrected in things around the person. Oliphant listed items that were known as prescriptions for relationships. "If your right shoe comes unlaced, someone is saying good things about you; left shoe—bad things. . . . Don't give your sweetheart a knife. It will cut your love in two."[10] In reading dreams and signs, the interrelated nature of the cosmos is highlighted. Human life is understood to be in relationship, part of the interconnected, shared web of the universe. Because humans and nature are understood as interrelated, it is possible to find ways to counter present or future negative life events and influences. The activities to counter the negative life events are called protection.

Again, in contrast to Oliphant's work, other researchers from Georgia edited their interviews in such a way that they shaped and interpreted the data they received, dropping healing into well-shaped narratives. In one account, the interviewer placed all healing into a medical model whereby outside doctors were part of the life of the enslaved:

All serious illnesses were handled by a doctor who was called in at such times. At other times Mr. or Mrs. Hale gave them either castor oil or salts. Sometimes they were given a type of oil called "lobelia oil." At the beginning of the spring season they drank various teas made out of the roots they gathered.[11]

Another researcher included a section from one interview on superstition rather than healing: "Bryant was not superstitious, although he did sometimes wonder when 'signs' proved true. Superstition, however, had a strong grip on slave life."[12]

Beyond Oliphant's and the Georgia Narratives, other interviews from other states include folk healing information. In the following excerpts, the concept of interrelationships between human and nature is evident.

Folk healing depends on the ability of the healer to draw on the power to control, protect, or attack, in short, to orchestrate the flow of the natural, the spiritual, and relational aspects of life. The power to do so is found in multiple places, including human or animal bodily fluids such as blood or saliva.

"Dey b'lieved dat an old person could punish anybody by taking a piece of chip and spitting on it and den dey would throw it on 'em. Dey said dat in two weeks time maggots would be in 'em."[13]

Natural elements are used, such as roots and salt. The practitioner learns to "work" the elements in order to draw power to achieve some desired end. Healing includes the preventative, in the same vein as holding a stick between the teeth while crossing a stream.

"Several of my informants say that salt can be used as a weapon of conjure."[14]

"Some of de roots dat dey used to brin 'em luck an' to trick foks wid was Rattle-Snake Marster, and John de Conqueror. John de Conqueror is supposed to conquer any kind of trouble you gits intuh. Some folks says dat you can tote it in your pocket an' have good luck."[15]

Animals such as lizards and black cats have power that can be accessed. Ritual assists in accessing such power.

"Another method used to fix or conjure people, according to Mrs. Rush, is to take a lizard and parch it. The remains must be put in something that the person is to eat and when the food is eaten the individual will be conjured."[16]

Conjuring served as a weapon, both offensively and defensively. One can protect oneself by "fixing" those who mean one harm, causing damage of some kind to those who are threats. Some of the former slaves' accounts noted the possibility of protection from beatings from overseers or owners.

"She [the conjurer] tol' me to put a piece of [a root] in my mouth an' chew it. When I got near de overseer I was to spit some of de juice towars him an' I would'nt git a whippin'."[17]

A definable spirituality operates in folk healing; it is closely aligned with African epistemologies. (Spirituality will be explored in greater detail later in the book.) Some might see deceased relatives, a phenomenon similar to ancestor veneration. Some might be believed to experience "witch riding," reminiscent of African stories of possession.

"The old folks b'lieved dat any house a person died in was 'hainted' and dat de dead person's spirit was a witch dat would come back at night. They used to put a pan of salt on de corpse to keep it fum purgin' and to keep de witches away."[18]

People who are born with cauls (a kind of veil) over their eyes will be able to see ghosts.[19]

Some characteristics of folk healing can be recovered from the Slave Narrative records. Yet, the aspects can become construction materials for a stereotype: many common views of folk healing become enmired in a simplistic view of African Americans, their ideas and practices, radically underestimating the intelligence and creativity they have employed. As the working definition of folk healing indicates, there are complex issues involved.

Hoodoo and Healing

The Slave Narratives introduce the terms "conjure" and "hoodoo." These terms need further explication. Hoodoo's historical development helps explain spiritual traits that take a holistic approach to folk healing. Hoodoo or conjure has a spiritual context: the individual is seen as grounded in community with relationships between humans and between self and the universe considered integral to their efficacy. As black religious historian Yvonne Chireau notes, religion "includes beliefs that are embedded in the ordinary experiences and deeply held attitudes, values, and activities of members of a group or community. . . . African American religion . . . encompasses noninstitutionalized expressions and activities."[20] This view assists in understanding folk healing in the widest frame possible.

An African-based spirituality informs hoodoo. Historically, in Protestant colonies of the United States, hoodoo or conjure masked the African practices forbidden under the European religious beliefs of those regimes. Africans in the United States found ways to adapt and hold on to spiritual practices. Historian Sterling Stuckey has identified the African roots of the slaves' religious expression in the ring shout, which "was, above all, devoted to the ancestral spirits, to reciprocity between the living and the dead."[21] The ring shout, involving the community performance of certain singing and dancing in a circle, could be found throughout the slave states and was infused in Christianized expressions of worship. Stuckey emphasized that the purpose of this shout was concealed from whites, as evidenced by the written comments of whites of the era. As a result, "[m]issionaries failed to halt African religion in Georgia because it took forms they did not understand or even recognize."[22] In the same manner, hoodoo was part of an African-derived spiritual consciousness, a way of transporting what was known into the alien situations of enslavement.

Hoodoo developed primarily in the Protestant southern slave states, where the enslaved Africans were unable to continue or to develop distinct religious forms that closely corresponded to African traditional religions. Slave codes in those states generally forbade practices such as drumming (centrally important in traditional African worship), which had the potential to develop clearly religious frames in the colonies, such as Voudou developed in Catholic Louisiana or Candomblé in Catholic Brazil. Hoodoo was not a formal religion, in contrast with Voudou. Hoodoo and conjure were able to stand quietly beside the Baptist, Methodist, and Anglican religions that forbade any "evil" practice that was deemed witchcraft in a way that overt practice of African religion could not. Hoodoo was pragmatic, revolving around roots and herbs for healing or protection, with a constant awareness of the interconnectedness of all life.

Practitioners of hoodoo receive informal training, learning first from others in the family or community. The conjurer has a sense of being self-taught, with an ability to intuit treatment. This intuitive aspect also comes from a feeling of being called to the practice. The beginner conjurer learns to collaborate with the divine order of the universe that connects that person to the community, nature, the past, and the present.

The conjurer could also be known as a rootworker because knowledge and use of plant life is part of the practice of conjuring. We will see these names used interchangeably in various accounts. Different writers concerned with the general subject of hoodoo will have similar definitions of the practice and its practitioners. For instance, a conjure woman, Menthy, is described in one account as a tall, "dark" woman, wise in the ways of ghosts:

> She might prescribe the sucking of alum, or rubbing the limbs with graveyard dirt. . . . For diagnosis Menthy will put a piece of silver in the hand or mouth of the sufferer. If the silver turns black, he has been conjured. . . . As a preventive against being tricked Menthy prescribes nutmeg worn on a string around the neck, or the red foot of a jay-bird carried in the pocket.[23]

Menthy's analysis of the state of illness and the use of natural objects for cures are seen in this short segment. The nutmeg and bird's foot are forms of charms. "Hands" (called thusly because they work) or mojos (a name of African origin) were the names of the charm bags worn by the person to effect magic. The conjurer uses the power drawn from these natural elements, often through ritual action. Common matters for which petitioners approach the conjurer include health, money, luck, and love. These could be to improve or block situations for oneself or others. For instance, the person who has been unable to get work or hold on to money may come to believe that he or she has been jinxed or fixed. The role of the conjurer is to uncross that situation. The people who seek the help of a conjurer are expected to pay something for services. Originally, the payment was less of an economics-driven supply-and-demand form of capitalism; rather, there was an African-based principle of spirituality, similar to tithing, that expects some return from those who are given a gift.

Menthy's methods included using a preventive against trickery. Protection is defensive and often involves a charm or mojo worn on the body. "Fixing" another person, where some kind of bad wishes are "thrown" on the person, is offensive. Again, natural elements, such as roots, stones, herbs, or animals, may be used to fix a person. In this account from the Slave Narratives, a narrator, Mr. Strickland, describes a method of becoming magical using a black cat:

> You boils 'im 'till he gits done all to pieces an' den you takes all de bones an' throws 'em in de creek an' de one dat floats up de creek is de one to use. You takes dis bone an' draws it through your teeth an' gits all de meat off an' den you can take dat bone an' do all kinds of majic. You can talk to folks an' dey can't see you. You can even disappear an' come right back. It takes a good 'un to do dat.[24]

The notion of a "good 'un" who might have power to disappear highlights folk tales about conjurers. The figure of the conjurer has captivated African American artistic imagination most notably in the classic work by Harlem Renaissance author Charles Chestnutt, *Conjure Woman,* or in the rendering of a conjurer in "The Conjur Woman" by twentieth-century artist Romare Bearden. In the 1930s, Zora Neale Hurston recorded folk tales about Uncle Monday and Aunt Judy Bickerstaff, both of whom had their own stories of power. However, they lived in the same area and became engaged in a professional competition that Aunt Judy ultimately lost.[25] The stories that Hurston told of these characters were colorful, capturing the sense of mystery that conjurers often represent in black communities.

Yet, on American soil, there have consistently been mixed messages and relationships in black communities about these conjurers. The conjurer can be viewed as powerful, someone who inspires fear, as in Hurston's Uncle Monday character. One white author identified the conjurers on plantations as both conservative and subversive, unable to break the control of the plantation owner but still powerful enough to make other slaves bow to his or her will. Fear was their primary weapon, the author declared. "Down to our time, hoodoo doctors, not being fools, have studied their people and learned how to provide them with advice designed to produce results an expensive psychoanalyst might envy."[26] Unfortunately, this view oversimplifies, turning all conjurers into evil people who use mind games on black populations.

Such interpretations are not limited to white authors. Essays by students at Hampton, a historically black college, that were written in 1878, negatively describe conjurers. "Powers of all kinds are attributed to these [conjure] doctors. The healing arts in various degrees is their gift, and the so-called 'diseases' which they possess exclusive power to cure are . . . tricks, spells and poison."[27] The skepticism of hoodoo's efficacy and denials of the conjurer's powers included a number of aspects. For some black people, the social need to establish distance from or discredit hoodoo was part of the processes of assimilation into white American society. There were also pressures from some church denominations for African Americans to become authentically Christian by rejecting anything that was deemed heathen, including the use of magic. Meanwhile, some of the conjurers discredited themselves by abusing their power or attempting to perform acts of power that were impossible.

The conjurer, despite negative reports, continued to figure in the black imagination. The idea of an individual with the power to mold human conditions and relationships, combined with an intimate knowledge of how nature works, taps into cultural concepts of the interconnectedness of life. Although the conjurer may seem to have dropped off the American mainstream's cultural landscape, a resurgence in twenty-first-century conjuring is evidence of the resiliency of the concept.

Information on healing or fixing was not solely the domain of the conjurer. Those who practice some form of conjure continued to operate in black communities. In addition to conjurers, designated healers or rootworkers were necessary for the life of the community and not easily discredited. There were few white doctors who would practice their medicine on African Americans during enslavement and for many years beyond Emancipation. This absence required the development of healers in and for black communities. Historian Deborah Gray White identified that healing the ill and nurturing infants were tasks given over to elderly enslaved women on plantations.[28] More specifically another researcher stated:

> In an era when bleeding and purging were the medical profession's accepted therapies for most varieties of disease and conditions, doctors looked to these practicing slave women for information on how to cure the diseases of the slaves and those of their owners as well. . . . Once obtained, the medical news was rapidly disseminated throughout the newly organized medical community of the United States—in medical publications, in medical education and in meetings of fledgling professional associations of white medical men.[29]

The need for the rootworker continued after the end of enslavement because racial segregation demanded that doctors or hospitals separate white clientele from African Americans. Although efforts of black clubwomen raised funds for black hospitals in urban settings such as Chicago, most African Americans in southern or rural areas had little access to this type of medical care. Instead, folk healers were known and trusted in their communities, establishing relationships with those who became their patients. Whether called rootworker or conjurer, folk healers continued to operate well into the middle of the twentieth century; then, state licensing of medical practitioners became law.

Concepts of conjure and rootwork often overlapped with faith healing. The idea that God gave the knowledge of what to do to take care of health problems emerges repeatedly in oral histories. One black woman who became a midwife in Alabama declared: "That was medication through faith healin. Whatever they'd use God led it through His knowledge and it worked because they didn't have nothing else to work with." She described seeing her sister being cured after having stepped on a hoe that cut to the bone. Their mother cleaned the cut and filled it with axle grease, even using other grease purchased from an itinerant peddler who sold cures. "Mother kep' it up. She kep' it clean. She didn't let no sand get in it and prayed and it healed. It healed. I'm talking bout what I looked at with these eyes. A miracle is the word."[30] There are similarities and overlaps in the descriptions of the sense of faith healing and folk healing. In faith healing, an accepted religious cause and motivation is assigned to the process of being healed. The healer is believed to be a conduit for Divine Power, such as Jesus or the Spirit. But some of the practices look very similar to those of the conjurer or rootworker, who is seen as accessing the power of nature, not specifically the Divine.

The role of faith healing in the religious lives of black people is supported by multiple testimonies of cures. Arthur Fausset noted one such instance in the historic text *Black Gods of the Metropolis*.

> Redeemed Love despaired of walking again. Someone said, "Father Divine!" The thought bore down upon her. Suddenly she was healed. Thus she became a Divinite. . . . C.C. believed that only through Daddy Grace could one get into the Kingdom. Naturally, also, Daddy Grace can heal the sick, and give sight to the blind.[31]

In black communities, conjuring and faith healing often make similar use of herbs and their applications for cures. The broad epistemological framework views nature, human, and the Divine as intimately related. Black community members generally do not see these forms of healing as discrete areas or different specializations. Instead, there is recognition of the gift of healing expressed in different ways.

Despite this common ground, there are many in black communities who disparage and distance themselves from forms of folk or faith healing, as we saw in the excerpt concerning the Hampton students. However, even their rejection of such ideas provides proof that the ideas still have currency in black communities: one cannot deny what one does not know. Despite some rejections, a mindset, reasoning process, and spirituality continued in black communities that remain grounding for folk healing to continue.

Healing: Through the Lens of Folklore

As we think back to the definition of folk healing delineated at the beginning of this book, we can see elements that are clearly discernable in the examples of the Slave Narratives of the preceding section. For African American folk healing, such description is needed to demonstrate the imbricated components that are part of its constructions. But the definition needs further elaboration.

Folk healing generally has been placed under the category of folk-lore. One folklorist, William Bascom, defined it thusly:

> Folklore means folk learning: it comprehends all knowledge that is transmitted by word of mouth and all crafts and techniques that are learned by imitation or example as well as the products of these crafts. . . . Folklore includes folk art, folk crafts, folk tools, folk costume, folk custom, folk belief, folk medicine, folk recipes, folk music, folk dance, folk games, folk gestures, and folk speech, as well as those verbal forms of expression which have been called folk literature but which are better described as verbal art.[32]

Bascom's definition provides that words, action, story, ritual, and practice all fall under the umbrella of folklore.

The designation of folklore itself becomes problematic because it is housed within multiple academic disciplines. Yet those who study folklore in English, literature, religion, cultural studies, or anthropology can attest its importance in the daily-lived community constructions of culture and identity. At the same time, the question of folklore's value beyond the aesthetic can be raised: is it only a novelty with little importance? Scholars across disciplines can attest that folklore makes and expresses meaning. There are several nuanced ways in which African American folk healing is a form of folklore.

The continuation of folk healing in black communities has been fed and supported by what one author termed "folk cultural associations":

> The hallmark of the folk cultural associations is that they are indigenous and autonomous groups, free to create their own social world. They are spontaneously generated by their members rather than consciously shaped and directed by an outside force. In their self-reliance, they draw on culturally derived innovations and an aesthetic fluidity based on African American folk cultural traditions. Moreover, the folk cultural equation and, to an extent, also the popular, ensures the persistence of African-based cultural adaptations.[33]

It is important to note that folk cultural associations can be formal or informal. Although there exist formal associations from family settings to church groups to lodges, the culturally derived innovations of cures and spells, along with traditions of healers, will be transmitted informally, perhaps part of side conversations at a meeting hall or workplace. The transmission process is an integral part of the "folk cultural equation."

African American folk healing relies on performance, which is integral to folklore. Stories of healers, those healed, or those witnessing a healing, commonly tell of the processes involved. Part of the role of the healer is to find a way, if there is nothing known, to develop the healing. Folk tales and myth become a form of communicating about the operations of the universe, human relationships, and, therefore, healing.

African American folk healing encompasses more than the physical dimension of the human person. The spiritual is seen as a realm in need of potential healing and can be considered sick, as indicated in the spiritual "Balm in Gilead," which, drawing from biblical phrases, emphasizes healing from a "sin-sick soul." Spirits also interact with the realm of the living, evidencing a cosmological view in which life continues after the death of the body, and the soul of the person continues to be involved in the world, sometimes for good, sometimes for ill. As another dimension of relationality, spirit possession in its many forms is a dramatic example of relationships between humans and spirits.

In African American epistemology, there is awareness of the related spiritual dimension and the intertwining of this life with the world beyond. These are also understood as being relational. Therefore, among many African Americans, spirituality is also a holistic practice: spirit and flesh, nature and humans, all are related and not understood as divorced from one another. Perhaps one reason that many African Americans feel so comfortable in so-called charismatic churches is their common shared sense of a spirit-filled world where God is an actor in daily life, accessible at any given moment. This holistic view does not mandate a list of rules but stresses relationships. Indirectly, an ethical vision of the good of human life and the aims of society are implied, as we will see in the following pages. Persons with the power of healing, speaking to spirits, speaking in tongues, or other charismatic gifts are seen to bear a certain responsibility to develop those gifts and to use them. Such gifts are themselves amoral and can be used for good or for evil. Responsibility for their use rests on the person, in conjunction with the community.

Folk healing, under the category of folklore, encompasses word, action, story, ritual, and practice. Black folk healing encompasses not only the individual but links between a person to community and cosmos. Relationality is central because folk healing in black traditions implies rightness in how "I" am to perceive "you." Healing itself is impersonal because the practitioner draws upon forces of nature. Even the power of the healer is perceived as impersonal, coming through one individual to another. There is no implied morality in African American folk healing; instead, the healing is amoral, depending on the intentions of the healer and those to be healed. The amoral aspect of folk healing places the burden of responsible use on the participants.

The healer must determine the cause of an illness as natural or unnatural. Natural illness is believed to result from exposure to cold, from misbehavior such as eating too much of a certain food, or from impurities that may be encountered in air or water. These illnesses have the potential of being treated with natural means, such as medicines. The idea of medicine in folk healing is not simply roots or spells. Sociologist Laura Jarmon has presented a definition of black folk medicine that highlights the concept's complexities:

> Medicines may be of any characteristic, from behavior to material form and from valued to disvalued intention; it may be natural or prepared, and it may function innately or by directive. Anyone and anything may participate in the operation of medicine, either directly or indirectly. Medicine is pervasive to the interests of participant groups that embrace it as a concept. Thus, broadly, all members of such groups practice medicines, from wearing a charm to rituals of birth, death, and propitiation. Medicine is institutional, represents accumulated wisdom and culture, and thus is attended by custodians who may be priests or other competents able to manipulate its force.[34]

Unnatural illnesses may also need healing but the concept requires more explanation. Simply put, causes of illnesses can be more than biological. For instance, relationships can be considered as a source of sickness, such as the results of an unhealthy marriage or worry over a child. One's own or others' bad actions or intentions can cause unnatural illnesses; this belief reflects African-derived concepts of the person who stands in relation to community, nature, and society. A person may also be hexed, fixed, or hoodooed by others. Evil the person may have done is also considered to result in illness. Each of these requires diagnosis and unnatural treatment by an expert such as a conjure woman or man.[35] In other words, treating causes, conditions, relationships, and spiritual malaise are all culturally part of African American experiences of healing.

One interviewee in the Works Progress Administration's Slave Narratives from the 1930s explained the power of unnatural illness. "Everytime somebody gets sick it ain't natchel sickness. I have seed folks die with what the doctors called consumption, and yet they didn't have it. I have seed people die with heart trouble, and they didn't have it. Folks is havin' more strokes now than ever but they ain't natchel."[36] Another interviewee pointed to the connection of unnatural illness with what seems to be mental illness. "Don't you one time believe that every pore pusson they has in the 'sylum is just natchelly crazy. Some was run crazy on account of people not likin' 'em, some 'cause they was getting' 'long a little too good. Every time a pusson jumps in the river don't think he was just tryin' to kill hisself."[37]

These ideas of folk healing have not been erased but have continued in black communities and among family members. Folk healing is embedded in black cultural patterns. Not merely a cultural artifact, healing practices also define something about black people, the power we have, and our spirituality. Such ideas stand in contrast with the quick dismissal given to healing practices as superstition or witchcraft. By its continuance, African American folk healing can be considered an alternative form of knowledge that black theologian Lee Butler names resistance culture. Resistance culture, Butler contends, is different from a popular culture that serves only the mainstream. Instead, culture as a form of resistance maintains a separate way of knowing in order to avoid dehumanization. Cultural resistance stands against the status quo.

> Standing against a rage that colorizes land rights, over-sexualizes sacred space, and racializes human dignity, the resistance culture declares its selfhood through what appears to be the outrageous, auda-

cious, unrehearsed presentation of sight and sound. . . . Its genius is often reduced to physical performance, which tends to be exploited and is assumed to be its only redeeming quality.[38]

African American folk healing is not a closed system; it is not frozen in time and it is not limited to a single place. Instead, African American folk healing is adaptable to different conditions and, like any aspect of a living culture, changes.

In African American communities, "wellness" may be a better descriptive term to use when discussing the aims of families and individuals in healing processes as opposed to the term "health." Wellness implies a temporary condition rather than a possession. "Wellness," rather than "health," aligns with the workings of black folklore, cultural traditions, and cultural resistance. "Wellness" references activity and goals rather than a finished product that is a commodity. Additionally, "wellness" serves to emphasize, by contrast, the way the word "health" is generally used in American medical culture and thereby stands in opposition to the commercialization of American medicine. Because it is less commonly used, "wellness" can more easily indicate a holistic view of what should be healed, aiming for wholeness and harmony.

Language: Representing and Being the "Folk"

Our topic is African American folk healing, but who are the *folk*? Knowing who are the folk identifies some root issues about characterizations of black folk healing. As hoodoo was differently defined by black and white Americans, so too were the designations of the folk historically based and distinct by racial group.

Throughout the history of the country, white Americans have generally depicted black people as questionable human beings: nonhuman or inherently flawed. The role of black Americans is, at best, perceived as the supportive sidekick for the white actor. Patricia J. Williams, a black feminist law professor, defines these boundaries:

And "blackness," of course, has been used as a most effective way of marking the African-American quest for either citizenship or market participation as the very antithesis: blacks are defined as those whose expressed humanity is perceived as "taking" liberties, whose submission is seen as a generous and proper "gift" to others rather than involving personal cost. The fraternal bliss of romanticized racism, in which professions of liberty and inseparable union could simultaneously signify and even reinforce an "American" national identity premised on deep social division is, again, the central paradox of our times.[39]

Language has been an important tool with which to identify black folk. The use and misuse of the "Negro" dialect in written folklore and narratives about folk healing maintained the differences from white Americans and discredited black thought as ignorant. Rhetorician David G. Holmes traced the development of dialect:

> While whites from the eighteenth to the early twentieth century were claiming a natural union between the physical appearance of blacks and their moral and intellectual ineptitude, the same assumptions were made on the basis of dialect. . . . Minstrel shows, invented by whites during the nineteenth century, supposedly afforded white audiences with a window into the collective souls of black people. . . . Black writers, such as [James Weldon] Johnson, accepted inadvertently a link between black dialect and African American identity.[40]

In sum, Negro dialect as developed by white people, kept black people wrapped in romanticized racism that turned them into the folk.

From the first use of literacy tests for voting, black Americans have been stamped as inferior goods in the United States because they employ vernacular language. Houston Baker Jr. points out how language has functioned to maintain sharply defined racial categories. He writes of the development of minstrelsy, but his conceptual framework can apply to the use of Negro dialect and serve as a guide for thinking about its meaning:

> By misappropriating elements from everyday black use, from the vernacular—the commonplace and commonly sensible in Afro-American life—and fashioning them into a comic array, a mask of *selective* memory, white America finds a *device* that only "counts" in relationship to the Afro-American systems of sense from which it is appropriated. . . . The device is designed to remind white conscious-

ness that black men and women are *mis-speakers* bereft of humanity
—carefree devils strumming and humming all day—unless, in a
gaslight misidentification, they are violent devils fit for lynching, a final exorcism that will leave whites alone.[41]

The performance of race, with and against this deformed view of
black people, Baker asserts, constitutes a significant portion of communication between black and white Americans. Baker's concept is
important because it illuminates the problem inherent in using much
written Negro dialect in contemporary work. Because many of the primary texts cited and quoted in this book were written in dialect, sift-
ing through some of the effects of this writing is imperative. The use
of some of these texts demands an exegetical task to ascertain the
meanings of the speakers despite the intent of and form used by the
writers.

If language had been a method for disenfranchising African
Americans in the past, it must be noted here that contemporary distancing also occurs. Although black dialect may have changed from
times of enslavement, there is still use of vernacular language among
African Americans. Black vernacular is today both mimicked and de-
cried. It is mimicked as it is commercialized in television ads or music.
Yet black vernacular continues to have a negative connotation in formal settings. Further, black vernacular is often subtly censured. For instance, the push for cultural "literacy" now connects reading levels
with nationalism, economic security, and patriotism. One example is
found in the late 1980s writings of E. D. Hirsch Jr.[42] about the importance of cultural literacy for every American.[43]

Language is clearly tied to the expression of black American folk
healing, and this aspect also underlines the use of the term "folk" in
this book. Language use is a key part of patterns of cultural resistance
as defined above. The use of language is integral in healing: words,
rituals, and dreams are constitutive of the methods of black folk healing. Action also has communicative and performative dimensions,
that is, language in itself.

The discussion of language brings African Americans' mixed responses to folk healing to the fore. Because of the relationships of black
Americans with wider American society and because of the oppressions and criticisms that black Americans have endured within the
national scene, as we have seen, some black people have consciously

distanced themselves and their families from "low" behavior such as use of the vernacular or folk healing that is deemed to reflect race.

Such distancing has historical antecedents, as is highlighted in the research of black feminist historian Evelyn Brooks Higginbotham. Vernacular expressions in black culture included the working-class and the blues cultures. Higginbotham traces how "the public emergence of a folk orality" developed as black people migrated from the South to the North in the 1920s and 1930s.[44] She specifically looks at how race records combined culture with consumerism, even while "validat[ing] the creative energies of the rural folk, turned urban proletariat, as an alternate, competing voice within African-American communities. At its most prosaic levels, the ascendant voice of southern folk culture challenged the middle-class ideology of racial uplift as pronounced by educated religious leaders of the late nineteenth century."[45] Consequently, Higginbotham contrasts ways that she views interpretations of black religious culture.

> Blues culture, working-class culture, and "blackness" become virtually synonymous. The religious culture of the working poor, when visible at all, appears as an anomaly or false consciousness. The blues and church are thus counterposed as cultural icons of class division. Perhaps this representation of working-class religion stems from the belief that African-American Christianity is white-derived, middle-class in orientation, and thus less authentically black. Or conversely, perhaps religion among the poor is not taken seriously because it is perceived as otherworldly, lower-class escapism, having no ideological implications and playing no strategic role in struggles over moral and cultural authority.[46]

Higginbotham's insights are important for this study of African American folk healing because folk healing is often valorized as authentically black, especially when or only when it appears related to a lower social class and when the language used is some black dialect. We discuss this notion of class in relation to African American folk healing in chapter 3.

The term—African American *folk* healing—is used to designate a location where black people continue to live everyday lives. "Folk" is a word that some theorists refer to historical peoples or a place in intellectual history where the term "*volkgeist*" was tied to romanticism.

The migration of African Americans from the South through the first half of the twentieth century became a moment when other black intellectuals applied a romantic brush to their migration struggles. David Nicholls asserts:

> As millions of black Americans left agricultural settings to pursue employment in urban centers, the *folk* seemed an appropriate term to describe these masses of former sharecroppers and farmhands who were moving across the landscape. Additionally, in homology with narratives of European national development, the folk provided the telos in narratives that sought to describe the development of the race into modernity.[47]

As the above excerpt indicates, built into discussions of "black folk" are questions of class. The folk were the migrants, the southern transplants to northern cities in search of work. Or the folk were the black people remaining in the South, especially those still bound to the land as agricultural workers. "Country" was generally considered by most African Americans in the North to be a negative designation from about 1920 through the 1970s. "Country" was a pejorative for a slow, ignorant, backward black person. To be acclimated to city life was usually considered a sign of sophistication, of becoming more "American" and farther away from the land-bound past of enslavement. Harlem, Los Angeles, or Chicago held industrial promises of wealth for the futures of black families that Charleston, Savannah, and Biloxi did not.

Occurring with these migratory shifts was a new diversification and distinction of black Americans. Never of a "peasant" class as in Europe, former slaves and former free blacks initiated new identities, even as white America continued to construct straitjacketed visions that denied difference. These stories and the migration of black folk healing concepts are taken up in chapter 3. Before turning to those stories and their implications, the contrasting contexts of black people in white-dominated American health systems are explored in chapter 2.

2

Healing, the Black Body, and Institutional Medicine

Contexts for Crafting Wellness

There are a good many folks carrying mojos around Alabama and Louisiana and Arkansas—you could fill the hold of a cotton boat with them. Some folks call them "greegrees." The conjur men who make them up put all kinds of things inside—dried blood, dirt from a graveyard, frizzled chicken feathers, dried-up bird feet, and things like that. I don't see nothing good about any of them. They all is fooling somebody.

—Excerpt from *The Big Old World of Richard Creeks*, 1962[1]

Frameworks for Healing from African American Perspectives

Healing is a culturally bound concept. Although there are larger societal frameworks, there are also intimate ones from particular cultures that inform individuals in dialogue with or despite the larger social structures. The operative frameworks for healing concepts among African Americans involve many intricately layered strata that are woven or blended together.

One layer of these understandings hearkens back to African cultural orientations. Anthropologists Sidney Mintz and Richard Price use the term "African cognitive orientations," which captures a sense of how "African-ness" was retained. The term recognizes that links between the past and present, between cultural realities and physical conditions, are not severed simply because of a change in location. Mintz and Price refer to African cognitive orientations as

[o]n the one hand, basic assumptions about social relations (which values motivate individuals, how one deals with others in social situ-

ations, and matters of interpersonal style), and, on the other, basic assumptions and expectations about the way the world functions phenomenologically (for instance, beliefs about causality, and how particular causes are revealed). We would argue that certain common orientations to reality may tend to focus the attention of individuals from West and Central African cultures upon similar kinds of events, even though the ways for handling these events may seem quite diverse in formal terms.[2]

These orientations infiltrate and influence African American understandings of health and healing. A closer look at a few dynamics of African understandings of the body, sexuality, and health and healing provides a backdrop for exploring connections with African Americans today.

In general, African understandings of the body perceive it "as the agent of concrete totality, radical identity, and ontological unity of the human being."[3] It follows, then, that spiritual values and meanings are reflected in the body itself. One expression of this idea is that differently shaped bodies, sometimes deemed a "deformity" in Western eyes, might instead be considered spiritually meaningful, depending on the African tradition. The body signals something about the spiritual life, encompassing the personal, familial, and communal in the present moment. More than that, the body connects the person to the ancestors and a new birth in a family may signal the return of an ancestral spirit.[4]

Through a holistic mindset, health and healing are related to religion and spirituality in African understandings. Health and healing are key values in African traditional religion, connected as they are with the fundamental theme of life. For many Africans, sickness is a diminution of life, and healing is a sacred activity second only to that of giving life.[5] The historian Albert Raboteau offers a statement of the African understandings of the interconnections of person, community and nature: "Africans conceived of the individual self . . . as constituted by a web of kinship relations. . . . Long before western medicine recognized the fact, African traditional healers stressed that interpersonal relations affected people's health."[6] This sense of unity of person and community is reflected in the concept of human being, particularly noted in the ways body and spirit are understood as related and unified. In this view, the human person is not a divided body and soul but a whole being. When the physical or spiritual are in conflict, illness of the body or relationships result. Likewise, a community can be deemed ill. A person or the community can be cured spiritually as well as physically.

Ideas from the African continent traveled to the United States with black people. The epistemological frameworks of people in Africa continued in the Americas and with good reasons. Social conditions of forced emigration to the United States, under the horrors of enslavement, insured that cultural retentions became crucial factors in survival. Colonization was enacted on black bodies in the American colonies.

Even without a one-to-one material correspondence, cultural patterns and concepts could be shared as enslaved people found commonalities. This cultural bonding was part of the transition of Ibo or Hausa, Gullah, or Creole, freed or enslaved, mulatto or quadroon into an eventual self-identification as *black* Americans. Cultural consciousness could become a factor that shaped black identity because it stood within a segregated system in which white Americans defined black bodies for their own purposes.

The retention of cultural orientations was an important part of enslaved black people's self-recognition of their own humanity. Bamidele Demerson, a curator at the Charles H. Wright Museum of African American History, begins his talks with students by asking a question: "If someone came in this room and took all of us to another place where we had never been before, we'd never return here, and we had nothing but the clothes on our backs—what would we have left?" The question causes students to struggle with the concept of what they *would* have without the things and people they know.

Demerson's question forces a practical reflection on the relationships of African Americans to African cultures, which has been debated in terms of *if* and *whether* enslaved Africans factually retained their cultures and the relationships to those cultures. Demerson's question forces recognition that human beings retain their senses of themselves and pass those on to their children, as much as possible, whether they provide exact sets of past practices or not. There has been much discussion and argument about the continuation of African patterns in black American life. Some will argue the absence of African connections, pointing to the physical severity, social oppression, or temporal distance of the enslavement period on black Americans as having prevented such links from surviving. Yet such views do not take into account the realities of black life: African Americans were physically under threat and socially segregated for much of their time on this continent.

In contrast to other immigrant groups to America, black people were legally and politically unable to obtain the economic and social benefits of citizenship. Yet, black workers, slave or free, significantly contributed to American growth and black people could see what was occurring. Like other oppressed people, they found ways to retain a sense of dignity and humanity. The connections to African ideas were not eliminated but provided a framework for survival and success. African cognitive orientations, in answer to the question Demerson posed, were significantly what the captured Africans brought with them. Folklore, for example, provided maxims for living. More than this, the connections to African ideas came to be defined as an area in need of healing along with identity, as will be discussed in chapter 5.

As a people separated from political and economic power, cultural retentions became counterclaims to signify their own humanity in the face of a system that denied it. Under enslavement, cultural retentions transparently make sense. Social ethicist Peter Paris describes the continuation: "Under conditions of slavery African Americans also maintained, in large part, their traditional understanding of person."[7] What may not be so transparent are cultural retentions after Emancipation. Considering that *Brown v. Board of Education*, the Supreme Court case ending legal segregation, was not until 1954; that the Voting Rights Act was not until 1964; that some states did not end legal prohibition against interracial marriage until the late 1990s; that some states and their villages still display symbols of the Confederacy; that social inequities separating black and white Americans yet remain: these are some indications that black cultural retentions indeed had significant functions.

The ways in which understandings of body and spirit among black Americans in the United States echo African concepts are complex and nuanced. As one example, African retentions can be recognized in black use of language. Earlier we discussed the creation of a Negro dialect as a sign of black ignorance in the white imagination. But while white folk were ridiculing black speech patterns, black folk were simply going about the business of creating alternative meaning spaces. They drew on African ideas about communication. Through individual words—such as "okay" and "geechee"—African words slipped into the American lexicon. Through music, black people created songs that used African rhythms to communicate their ideas. These songs translated into original American music styles, from blues to jazz. Communication also happens through symbols, such as the designs of traditionally patterned black quilts, designs that can be traced to Africa. One communication pattern that can be traced directly back to the African continent is that of orality. The griot kept the community's stories, or folk tales taught lessons: the art of storytelling has shaped meaning and kept histories for black communities.

Even as these African roots can be located, African Americans continue to find ways to carve out clearly identified spaces wherein their humanity is honored. In other words, black people use their cultures to respond to the situations of their American lives. Because white people constructed race and racism, creating situations to which black people must respond, views based on experiences of oppression will occur. The difficulties of discussing black bodies in positive ways from within black communities, while standing against white scorn, are related to folk healing retentions. The resulting discussions of bodies demonstrate how attempts to vindicate African Americans' humanity might shape black concepts of body, sexuality, healing, or illness. For instance, some African Americans believe that the African American body is shaped differently by virtue of African heritage. One black author, Linda Villarosa, writes,

> African-Americans may carry a specific gene from our African forebears that predisposes some of us to excess weight, according to Lorraine Bonner, M.D., a physician who practices on Oakland, California. "There is evidence to suggest that the Africans who survived the Middle Passage to this country were those who were best able to utilize and retain the meager scraps of food they were fed. . . . People who are in an environment of famine maintain fat as a means of selective survival."[8]

This statement represents a kind of folk wisdom that justifies the body shape and weight of African Americans, especially given the high obesity rates in black communities. But this argument excludes some basic data: many people still on the African continent or in other Diasporic countries do not demonstrate such high rates of obesity.

Thus, the presumption that fat is a black genetic predisposition seems not to be supported by the evidence. And what about genetic heritage that is derived not from African lineage but from European, Native American, Asian, or other cultural lines? Such selective arguments arise to counter racism. They are helpful for learning how people act to survive and diminish insecurities that may be imposed by larger cultural biases; they are not good bases on their own for developing clear understandings of the complexities of race and culture.

The feeling that a defense of a different or larger body type is necessary arises from repeated exposure to commercially produced white ideals of physical perfection—thinner lips or skinnier hips—that can lead toward a perilous thinness. Conversely, the differences in body shape can become something celebrated by black communities. Author Alice Walker emphasizes: "[W]e don't have a tradition of skinniness in any sense—not in our food, not in our bodies. The sense of roundness . . . is a very precious thing we share with the majority of peoples in the world. The whole thing about being angular and linear . . . it's not our culture, it's not our tradition."[9] Despite such defenses, the pressures to conform to commercial standards of beauty add to the layers of complexity around African American understandings of the body today.

The different ways that African Americans consider the concepts of illness and healing are related to their conceptualizations of the body. One woman's discussion of her survival of cancer exemplifies the differences; she testifies that "Words conjure," and asserts that cancer is a conjuring word. She defines her existence between her experiences of chemotherapy as "This ain't really me. . . . This is just my flesh." By facing her mortality, she is able to live more peacefully, enjoying every moment. "Cancer is indeed a *conjuring* word. But its power comes from our fear. I have faced death and I know when my time comes, whether I am stalked slowly by cancer, or hit swiftly by a Mack truck, I am clear. Those are things that might happen to my body, but my spirit will rise victorious."[10] In this brief excerpt, she personifies death and cancer, defines a relationship between her body and soul, and uses "conjure" as a descriptive word. As with the discussion of the body, this woman uses language as a tool to combat her situation. Healing is performed and a story is told in an African style.

The ideas expressed by one woman give glimpses into the complexities of African American constructions of spirit and healing. The intricate relationships between African cultures and black Americans or between healing and language are not isolated but refer to an entire process of selecting and constructing identity. One author demonstrates how similar processes can be identified in the creation of black political cultures. He examines folk tales, proverbs, and church affiliation; he often finds that resulting black political behavior was "complex and at times contradictory." The way messages are brought to black communities are also critical in political decision making. Most important, "Style is in itself a statement of identity and an assertion of freedom."[11] Likewise, with folk healing: language, the conjurer, understandings of the black body—realistic or not—all constitute stylistic layers of identity and an assertion of freedom.

Among the areas already discussed, spirituality is a particularly salient realm in which some African orientations are retained. In religiosity, folk healing most clearly crosses and weaves African with black American cultures. The dynamic interplay of religion with healing traditions is a story that begins with the arrival of Africans on these shores. Black theologian Will Coleman has traced the religious dimensions of African traditions through the enslavement period. He posits the idea that the West African belief system was not ended with enslavement but modified, and is discernible through analyses of black religions:

> Throughout the Americas, Voodoo (Haiti and New Orleans), Hoodoo (Southern United States outside of New Orleans, Obeah and Myal (Jamaica), Santeria (Cuba, Puerto Rico), Macumba, Candomblé, and Umbanda (Brazil) combined African elements with Native and Euro-American folk beliefs, strains of European Gnosticism, and the Christianity of the Euro-Americans (Catholic and Protestant) to form religious systems that suited the needs of an African Diaspora.[12]

The conjurer was part of this spectrum of enslaved Africans' religious life and belief. Conjurers developed healing strategies "that would have been consonant with that of their West African ancestors. In this sense, nature herself unfolded like a textbook whose pages were disclosed for the interpretation and application of the combination of ingredients best suited for a particular ailment."[13]

This epistemological framework for healing influences black Americans today to varying degrees. Both health and spirituality texture the lives of African Americans and denote hopes for personal wholeness, for some cohesion of the fragments of personal life and community. This mindset values the cessation of oppressions and healing of social divisions. At the same time, African Americans are influenced by the views of white Americans, which often temper these traditional conceptual frameworks, imposing denigrating beliefs on black Americans. In light of this influence, one author is moved to state, "African peoples must eliminate the contradiction of seeing themselves through the eyes of others."[14] This includes the sometimes conflicted ways that African Americans view their bodies. The next section turns to an analysis of this phenomenon.

The Black Body in the U.S. Context

The questioning of the humanness of people of color by white Americans was chillingly pragmatic; black bodies, after all, were imported as labor and designated as investment property with no rights to participate in the society of the United States. The process of making slaves has been referred to as "seasoning" black people into positions of servitude. The horror of the process is described in detail in various sources.[15] The many effects of shaping black people into chattel slaves included instilling various untruths about their humanity. Black bodies were "read" from white cultural perspectives:

> For their suitability for slavery, [and] how to imagine blackness into meaning, how to see solutions to their own problems in the bodies of the slaves they saw in the market. Gazing, touching, stripping, and analyzing aloud, the buyers read slaves' bodies as if they were coded versions of their own imagined needs—age was longevity, dark skin immunity, a stout trunk stamina, firm muscles production, long fingers rapid motion, firm breasts fecundity, clear skin good character. The purposes that slaveholders projected for slaves' bodies were thus translated into natural properties of those bodies—a dark complexion became a sign of an innate capacity for cutting cane, for example.[16]

These political motives linked with academic and religious communities to develop justifications for the state of black bodies. Developing disciplines of ethnography and anthropology through the late eighteenth and nineteenth centuries, for instance, went hand in glove with colonialist politics. Colonialist actions were informed and supported by the theories of the day. Questions of the humanity of black bodies drew from a potent combination of philosophies from Jean Jacques Rousseau to John Locke; were infused with European beliefs in Progress and related definitions of civilization and culture; were buoyed by the growth of nationalism and the practices of capitalism; reinforced by development of theories of evolution; and blessed by the placement of Science and Reason as the new, improved, verifiable gods of modern thinking.[17]

For instance, in the early nineteenth century, Samuel Cartwright was a medical doctor in New Orleans who rendered his scientific opinion on the race of black humans:

> The blackness of the prognathous race, known in the world's history as Canaanites, Cushites, Ethiopians, black men or negroes, is not confined to the skin but pervades, in a greater or less degree, the whole inward man down to the bones themselves, giving the flesh and blood, the membranes and every organ and part of the body, except the bones, a darker hue than in the white race.[18]

The establishment of the colonizers' Christian theological perspectives through the eighteenth and nineteenth centuries buttressed the justification of enslavement by physical, racist mythologies. These perspectives simultaneously proved that God wanted black people enslaved and that God had created white people as superior. In 1856, one Baptist minister cited his biblical proof that God condoned slavery: "God raised up a succession of prophets to reprove that people [Israelites] for various sins into which they fell; yet *there is not a reproof uttered against the institution of involuntary slavery, for any species of abuse that ever grew out of it.*"[19]

More than a justification of enslavement, Christianity was intimately a part of the growth of black-as-inferior arguments, with white theorists developing negative views of black folk and black activist intellectuals strongly refuting such claims. Two writers of the mid-1800s, one black and one white, illustrate this point. In Boston in 1829, David Walker published *Appeal to the Coloured Citizens of the World*, advocating an end to enslavement. Walker, a black man, based his arguments on Christian scripture and advocated that those who were enslaved should overthrow their purported owners. He drew heavily from the story of the Exodus of the Hebrews from Egypt. The success of rebellion was under God's care:

> Fear not the number and education of our enemies, against whom we shall have to contend for our lawful right; guaranteed to us by our Maker; for why should we be afraid when God is, and will continue . . . to be on our side? The man who will not fight under our Lord and Master Jesus Christ, in the glorious and heavenly cause of freedom and of God . . . ought to be kept . . . in slavery. . . . Are we MEN!—I ask you, O my brethren! Are we MEN? Did the creator make us to be slaves to dust and ashes like ourselves?[20]

Walker clearly advocated an equality of humans under God, for which enslavement was an evil to be corrected, by force if necessary. Walker's writing, naturally, upset whites, particularly in the South, where legislation was developed banning his text and a bounty of at least $3,000 was supposedly issued for Walker himself.[21]

Walker's and other such views were buried under an avalanche of politically sanctioned writings by whites that promoted the lowered state of black life, using the Bible as theological proof. The medical doctor Samuel Cartwright had no qualms about drawing upon his theological views as a form of evidence for his medical pronouncements.

> The verb, from which his Hebrew name is derived, points out this flexed position of his knees, and also clearly expresses the servile type of his mind. Ham, the father of Canaan, when translated into plain English, reads that a black man was the father of the slave or knee-bending species of mankind. Who knows but what Canaan's mother may have been a genuine Cushite, as black inside as out, and that Cush, which means blackness, was the mark put upon Cain? Whatever may have been the mark set upon Cain, the Negro, in all ages of the world, has carried with him a mark equally efficient in preventing him from being slain—the mark of blackness.[22]

Although legal enslavement ended in the mid 1800s, the years since have witnessed a continued search for ways to marginalize African descendants in America while benefiting from their labor. Even so,

Walker was not alone in framing arguments against these racist constructions. Other intellectuals, black and white, analyzed and rejected such beliefs. In the nineteenth century, African American Anna Julia Cooper advanced one of the first arguments to understand the social construction of race, class, and gender: "Race, color, sex, condition are realized to be the accidents, not the substance of life, and consequently as not obscuring or modifying the inalienable title to life, liberty, and pursuit of happiness."[23] In the twentieth century, black social critic and sociologist W. E. B. Du Bois provided deeper analysis, which understood race as humanly constructed rather than biological or divinely decreed. "Race is a cultural, sometimes an historical fact. And all that I really have been trying to say is that a certain group that I know and to which I belong, as contrasted with the group you know and to which you belong . . . bears in its bosom just now the spiritual hope of this land because of the persons who compose it and not by divine command."[24]

Two white anthropologists in the early twentieth century, Franz Boas and Melville Herskovits, rejected notions of the inferiority of people of color, based on the developing discipline that was important in analyzing race. However, these counterviews were often deemed to be aberrations or oddities rather than part of the legitimate canon of Western thought. Further, they were bounded by the beliefs of the time, as well as the unexamined perspectives of race, gender, and class. At the center of this discussion are the ways that black bodies were constructed in the white American imagination: useful, expendable tools but of questionable humanity. "Whoever controls the images of a people or a culture is crucial to the domination and identity of that people or culture. The images of blacks have been largely shaped, controlled, and nourished by beliefs about blackness within the dominant cultures of Europe and America."[25]

Beyond enslavement, the continued social construction of black bodies to be perceived as inferior was held firmly in place with the use of technologies of racism, as Sara Chinn points out. Eugenics, biology, statistics, and race science combined with moralizing to "make" bodies that conformed to stereotypical views and labeled as scientific evidence. "These developments soldered together sets of subordinated bodies that were dehumanized and silenced by the joint discursive powers of the law, scientific inquiry, and medical research. Bodies were both de- and hypercorporealized: reduced to elements in a statistical model, and rendered visible only as a collection of physical features (skin color, hair texture, and so on)."[26] Medicine, as it was developing among white scientists, became one more technological facet. "For the medical profession the body became a Frankenstein's monster *avant le coup*: a collection of parts each one of which the surgeon could detach, reattach, delve into, and bring into view *as* parts."[27]

Jim Crow laws continued to impose legal separation of races until the Civil Rights Acts of the 1960s. In the years since, an equitable balance between black and white Americans has not been achieved. Not only is there a lack of economic parity but political and social inequities are also fueled by continued marginalization of black Americans. Black economist Marcellus Andrews contends that the foundation for civil rights reforms was created in a time of economic well-being, and insuring rights for one cohort would have potential benefits for both. But as economic times have become harder, black Americans' social and political advancements would come at the expense of white Americans; therefore, such reform has become unpopular.[28]

Through changing political and social fortunes, African American bodies remain mythologized in the American mind. Considering black bodies as somehow different assists in marginalizing black people. For instance, black men's bodies are set up as fear-inspiring potential criminals.[29] However, black men's strength is considered in a positive way if channeled into spectator sports. The possibilities of social and economic success as a sports star subtly encourages black boys in particular to engage in grade school and high school sport competitions at the expense of academic work. In this as in other arenas, the black body is turned into a commodity, offered up to labor at entertaining audiences.

Religiously and socially defining black bodies was inherited from the era of enslavement; segregation by law or practice was a primary factor in the continuing negative definitions of black people. Such definitions, together with black cultural patterns, enabled the milieu in which the continuation of African American folk healing was created. Today, alternative healing practices are not quirky cultural artifacts that have lingered among black Americans. Despite real or imagined social advances, the majority of African Americans are still at the bottom rungs of social, economic, and political ladders. Folk healing practices, not only for the good of the physical body but also for the emotional and spiritual aspects of the individual or community, have never had the impetus to atrophy in black life. Folk healing has gone underground or taken new forms but has not disappeared from the black cultural landscape. Recognizing race and racism and their development along historical trajectories supplies key contexts for understanding the continuation of black folk healing.

The way that race is constructed in the United States sets it up to continually trump cultural distinctions between and among black people. Toni Morrison baldly states: "I have never lived, nor has any of us, in a world in which race did not matter."[30] Mainstream America usually posits a monolithic black "culture" as diversity among African Americans is reduced to stereotypes, like Sambo or Mammy. This diminution of a people's complex culture into types limits social acceptance and mobility.

Folk medicine has most often flown under the radar of racist technologies. Those who see black folk healing only as the best-forgotten remnants of superstition have often ignored it. Black nationalists may hold it up as a kind of innate intelligence, turning black folk healing into another form of black vindication. Neither perspective recognizes the layers of exchange between races, cultures, political worlds, and intellectual traditions.

Black women and men hold complex, culturally based, survival-oriented views of life, which inform conceptualizations of body and spirit, of options for health, and of expectations for healing. In these structures, folk healing has its context. These frameworks for healing include consideration of African remnants underlying black American thought and the idea of the *folk*. These points provide an understanding of the locations from which black Americans craft the wellness that all the forms of folk healing offer.

Institutional Medicine and Black Folk Healing

The term "institutional medicine" sharply distinguishes folk healing from medicine and medical practice, a multibillion-dollar business in America that operates as an industry. When new drugs come to market, the announcement is largely a matter for Wall Street. Drug producers hawk their wares on television commercials. Drug sales representatives woo doctors' offices. Legislators and lobbyists determine the shape of the industry. HMOs, PPOs, and other forms of health insurance pay all or part of the costly bills for service. Yet millions of Americans are without adequate health care insurance and therefore have no access to institutional medicine. Medical training often demands a distancing of the health care professional from those seeking their services. In the context of institutional medicine, individual persons are treated for symptoms that are usually taken out of the contexts of their lives in the labyrinthine systems that constitute American health care.

Physician Howard F. Stein defines the medical model as "American society's dominant clinical framework for conceptualizing and treating issues that are subsumed under the rubric of disease. Under this model, the physical body and its constituent parts are the units of clinical discourse."[31] Under this model, biomedicine (which he contrasts with ethnomedicine) operates with its own culture and value system. "From the viewpoint of first-order biomedical values, caring, comforting, non-directive counseling, waiting, and 'doing nothing' are anathema. Actively intervening, aggressively treating, controlling, curing, and fixing the patient are acceptable and are sources of increased self-esteem for the clinician. The latter core values preserve the illusion of distance between healer and patient."[32]

In the biomedical culture, disease is considered abnormal, which establishes the role of the sick person.

> Illness is a form of deviance, both statistically and functionally, from the normal. Treatment is a rite of social control which purpose is to restore to functional normalcy the disequilibrium in relationships of all concerned, although a designated patient may be the focus of the ritual process. The patient if permitted by family, medical professionals, and society at large to enter the sick role and temporarily abdicate normal role obligations. The understanding remains, however, that the patient will participate diligently in the treatment process, respond to medical efforts in his or her behalf, and recover and reassume his or her conventional social roles.[33]

An overheard remark of a black nurse voices another, nonmainstream perspective on these ideas. She stated that doctors treat and mask symptoms and manage disease rather than offer cures. This brief observation presents a distinction from folk healing and an added motivation for African Americans to remain distant from institutional medicine.

Near the end of enslavement, and through and beyond the years of Reconstruction, African Americans' sociopolitical lives and the development of institutionalized medicine intertwined. Because African Americans were considered social outsiders, they were too often viewed as potential subjects for scientific experiments. At the same time, following Emancipation, many black Americans desired acceptance and participation as full citizens, including the possibilities of attending medical or other professional schools.

An example of these complex relationships is found in a story of a medical experiment at Tuskegee Institute in Alabama. Several hundred black men with syphilis believed they were being treated through a special medical program. But that did not happen during the forty years—1932–1972—of the program's existence. Instead the men were used as guinea pigs to collect data on the long-term effects of untreated syphilis. But why at Tuskegee, a black institution? There had been a strong effort by black leaders such as Booker T. Washington to develop a public health movement among African Americans. With Washington's central role at Tuskegee, the institute was prominent enough to warrant the questionable honor of hosting the experiments.

The Tuskegee Institute was a readily identifiable center of concern about black health issues by both black and white communities. One sign of its community presence was evident in the work of the Tuskegee Movable School in Macon County, Alabama, at the beginning of the twentieth century. The Movable School began in 1906 as a mule-drawn wagon that carried agricultural information to the black farmers in the fields. By 1915, female home demonstration agents were added to promote good housekeeping practices for rural black women. "The underlying philosophy of home demonstration work was that, even if poor rural women could not buy modern conveniences, they could still enjoy the appearance of modern consumer culture."[34]

One of the home demonstration agents was Eunice Rivers (later Eunice Rivers Laurie), the nurse who became instrumental in the recruitment and follow-up of the subjects in the "Tuskegee Study of Untreated Syphilis in the Negro Male." In the late twentieth century, Rivers was a central character in a book and a movie about the study.[35] But she was not alone as a black health professional involved in or aware of the study.

> Dr. Eugene Dibble, the black medical director of the Tuskegee Institute and head of its hospital, had given his approval to the study from its inception and had also performed some of the spinal punctures and autopsies on the men. Dr. William Perry, a black physician from the Harvard School of Public Health, sanctioned the study and participated in it. Dr. Jerome J. Peters, a staff physician at the Veterans Hospital in Tuskegee, likewise performed spinal punctures and autopsies on the men. In 1969, nearly thirty-seven years after the study began, most in the predominately black medical establishment in Macon County had sanctioned the study.[36]

The aims of many black women and men in institutional medicine were the growth and development of black public health. The good of black communities was most likely in their minds as they hoped to lead black Americans into greater acceptability among white society, to end discrimination, and to eliminate health problems. "Black professionals . . . did not protest the syphilis study because they saw it directing federal attention toward black health problems—a primary goal of the black public health movement."[37] Eunice Rivers Laurie defended her role in the study as reflecting the mindsets of black people then in institutional medicine.

> First, Rivers argued that the effects of the experiment were benign. In her mind it was important that the study did not include people who had early syphilis because those with latent syphilis were potentially less infectious. . . . Second Rivers accounted for her participation by stating that the study had scientific merit. . . . Finally, based on the available health care resources, Rivers believed that the benefits of the study to the men outweighed the risks.[38]

For Rivers, participating in professional health care could provide a change in perceived social status. For people trying to find a way "up," becoming a doctor or nurse could serve very well. The Tuskegee study was never a secret; there were several published reports that would have been available to medical professionals. In April 1958, Rivers herself was lauded for her work:

> Eunice Rivers became only the third recipient of the Oveta Culp Hobby Award, the highest commendation given to an employee of the Department of Health, Education and Welfare. The citation read, "[F]or notable service covering 25 years during which through selfless devotion and skillful human relations she has sustained the interest and cooperation of the subjects of a venereal disease control program in Macon County, Alabama."[39]

Yet many of the conflicts in the public health balancing act continued to revolve around questions of the humanity and expendability of black people. Such negative attitudes and conflicts led to the justified existence of less-frightening folk medicine.

This set of experiences of institutional medicine, and the relationships of African Americans within it, alone cannot explain the continuation of folk healing in black communities. A volume of 1970s essays considered many aspects of folk healing. One of the authors stated:

> But it [folk healing] isn't completely dead. Although these practices are not much in evidence in modern American cities (and the majority of American's population—white and black—lives in urban centers now), there are occasional reports that suggest some of the old power is still there, that it still influences behavior in significant ways. Though fewer people may be involved in the various levels of practice than in previous years (as is the case with most rural folk traditions brought to the city), many still take them with as much seriousness as ever, with deadly seriousness. Both folk remedies and the techniques for control still surface as significant elements in certain communities.[40]

This author continued on to analyze late-nineteenth-century oral histories and admitted the limited continuation of folk healing practices in "certain" black communities. "There were few other sources of power available to the slaves and ex-slaves; there was no justice in the courts for them and no regular source of financially reasonable medical aid from the white doctors in town."[41] This author strongly implies that the lack of social power and available institutional medicine is the only reason for folk healing's continuance. Others also analyzed folk healing as anachronistic.

One physician, who contributed to the same 1970s volume, emigrated to the United States from Germany in 1936.

> These findings confirmed that nine rusty nails in a pint of whisky, possibly "shine," is still a widely used home remedy. So is clay eating for 'treating the worms' and starch eating for an easier pregnancy. New to me was the drinking twice daily of a tea brewed from Spanish moss to supplement the insulin injection required by a twenty-five year-old Negro—a true blending of scientific and folk medicine.[42]

He held a clearly liberal view of multiple encounters with folk medicine in his own and others' medical practices. Yet this same doctor indicated that folk healing would go away with time, and he struggled intellectually to reconcile folk healing to biomedicine:

> Folk medicine is surely not dead. It has been more and more replaced by aspirin, vitamin supplements, tranquilizers, pep pills, and The Pill. . . . Today too many people live in the gray zone of quackery, plain hoax, and humbug. The relationship of folk medicine and scientific medicine is truly a two-way street. Folk medicine has one advantage: it has no doubt; it believes. Scientific medicine moves from truth to error to truth—it must search and research.[43]

The authoritative placement of institutional medicine in America today might have spelled the demise of folk healing practices among African Americans. The numbers of black people employed as professionals in institutional medicine seemingly could invalidate folk practices. Yet, as we have seen in our discussions of racial segregation and black misinterpretation, these have helped to maintain cultural groundings that support folk healing.

The cost of institutionalized medicine is a factor for consideration. Has cost alone made the difference in the retention of black folk healing? The cost of institutional health care is tied to its availability and quality in black communities. Hospitals and doctors are not generally viewed as trustworthy in black communities, as evidenced by such past events as the Tuskegee experiments. Black Americans' understandings of spirituality, their bodies, and healing are neither understood nor respected by these same hospitals. Racism is still experienced by patients while being treated in the hospitals in black communities, and the hospitals that have remained open seem to offer a lower quality of service than is found in whiter, wealthier communities. Black people know how these realities affect their health care options. When considering where to get help, hospitals are not necessarily the first places to which African Americans turn. It is not merely the cost of institutional medicine but the shape of biomedical culture that has become a consideration in black health care decisions. To imagine that folk healing continues to exist only because black people do not have money or health insurance is too simplistic. Folk healing held on because it has value and efficacy among African Americans, in contrast to institutionalized medicine. When African Americans obtain college degrees in medical professions, many are finding ways to honor their culturally based views of bodies and healing, particularly if they work in black communities.

One black woman I interviewed is a case in point. She has an advanced degree in nursing and still finds ways to connect folk practices with her education and training.

> When I think about . . . holistic medicine and . . . herbs and using some alternative therapy, I've always seen myself as a person that thought that was a neat idea. And I've always dabbled in that—I've never really studied it in detail. [I tell my paying clients in my home health care business], if they say this herb seems to help, I say, "Well, let's combine this with [your regular medicine] and see if that helps." I kind of think we can blend the two.[44]

This woman's words give evidence of the continued importance of a folk healing mindset, even in new forms, among African Americans. Often, that continuation is furthered and supported by well-educated black people like this nurse who find ways to link the past with the present.

Although repeated demonstrations of some forms of folk healing in the twenty-first century constitute the second half of this book, there is another part of the foundations of black folk healing to consider first. The next chapter explores elements that give folk healing resiliency in black communities.

3

Healing in Place

From Past to Present

A hard head makes a soft behind.
Little pitchers have big ears.
I'm not fattening frogs for snakes.
Don't measure my apples in your half-bushel.
*In every garden there is a snake—the bigger the garden, the more
    snakes.
*Pretty is as pretty does—not how pretty looks.
*Keep livin'—just keep livin'.
                —African American folk sayings; those with an asterisk are
                        by courtesy of Maurice, also known as "Bull"

The movements of African Americans from the South to the North and West in the mid-twentieth century contain stories of how black American cultures were retained over time and space. Some of these retentions can be found in folk sayings, as above. These sayings helped define relationships and how to carry on in the world. The sayings hold the germ of a black epistemology that identifies the interconnections between humans and nature and one another. I contend that African Americans have retained folk healing practices into the twenty-first century. Reflecting on my family assists my initial understanding of how these practices were carried across generations. My father was of the first generation of his family from the South. My mother's family had been in the North for several generations. My father's "countrified" practices and family were sometimes an embarrassment for her. But both sides of the family carried cultural healing practices that were infused into daily life along with other folkways. Even so, it could still be asked: why hasn't folk healing died out among black Americans? Chapter 1 brought forward the voices from the Slave Narratives, recorded in the 1930s but drawing from a history of enslavement. Chapter 2 deepened some of the underlying concepts. To understand the retentions of African American folk healing into the present day requires a closer look at the second half of the twentieth century.

The Great Migrations and Northern Experiences

When I interviewed Ms. Essie, she was 103 years old with seven children and twelve grandchildren. Her life story includes experiences of the Great Migrations, which were the movements of black Americans from the South with its sharecropping and lynchings to northern industrial centers. These patterns of migration were different from the movement that immediately followed Emancipation, when black people moved away from the sites where they had been enslaved. At the turn of the century, there was hope for new beginnings of economic growth and security. In 1895, Booker T. Washington gave what is called his "Atlanta Compromise" speech at the Cotton States Exposition, urging black Americans to "cast down their buckets" where they were and find ways to build futures in the South. Despite his pleas, thousands of black Americans traveled north and west through the early years of the twentieth century, searching for better lives. Chicago, Detroit, Gary, and other cities held out the prospect of employment in booming industries, auto manufacturing for one. These metropoles can trace the growth of their black populations to these migration patterns. As people traveled, black cultural referents, including folk healing, were carried from one environment to another.

Shifts to northern urban centers redefined black communities' shapes. At the same time, many African Americans retained their southern familial connections, often thinking of Alabama or Georgia as "home" generations later. Developing a solid sense of racial and cultural identity was important for the migrants to make new connections while feeling grounded.

Ms. Essie's story is one of many shared by southern migrants. She married at a young age, as did many rural women at the beginning of the twentieth century. She and her husband tried sharecropping in Mississippi, the first year planting cotton and corn but not making any money. When the owner told them, "Y'all just broke even, you can borrow all the money you want," the young couple could see the futility of continuing to farm through a sharecropping system. Ms. Essie's husband borrowed the money, which became their "get away" money. He left Essie, cautioning her to not tell the "old rider" that he had gone, to go into the field and act as if she were chopping cotton. "So I would go out there and piddle around. One day the old rider come along and said, 'What you doing out there, trying to use the farm yourself? You can't do nothing with that farm.'" Eventually, her husband sent for her, so she and her sister-in-law packed their belongings and some food, and got on a train to Chicago. After following her husband to different Midwest cities in search of work, they eventually settled in Michigan in 1916.

Obtaining "get away money" to reach the North, where factory work held the promise of regular paychecks, became an objective for many black southerners. The southern system of strict segregation was enforced by white political and economic power structures backed by fear of lynchings and other hate crimes and became strong motivation for black people to move elsewhere. The numbers of black Americans who left the South tell the story. Sociologist Stewart Tolnay notes the numbers on different levels. In 1910, 50 percent of black southern households were farms; in 1960, 10 percent. In 1910, 89 percent of black Americans resided in the South; in 1970, 53 percent. Tolnay stresses the significance of the shift from rural to urban living and the impact on black social structures.[1]

Ford Motor Company had several sites in Michigan available for unskilled black laborers, in particular the plants at Willow Run and Detroit. Company founder Henry Ford established links with black pastors in southern states through whom he recruited "good" black men—i.e., those who would work hard and not challenge the system. The swift growth of black populations impacted the shape of northern cities' communities. For instance, Detroit's 1910 African American population was a little more than 1 percent; by 1960, it had grown to 28.9 percent.[2]

But the northern cities and industrial complexes were not an end to experiences of racism. Rather, different forms of racist experiences waited. Black Americans began to refer to the North as "up South." A 1907 advertisement for a Negro conference in Philadelphia stated:

[There is a] growing tendency to enact legislation restricting the rights and privileges of colored citizens, and the increasing discriminations, which are being made against them in almost every field of honest labor—that the race situation in this country is grave and abnormal beyond measure, and that it is in some respects becoming worse and worse with each succeeding year.[3]

Black Americans in the South recognized the barriers and the racism they would face, but generally saw the North as the real land of opportunity. A black educator in New York in the early 1900s, William L. Bulkley, gave a speech that analyzed the effects of racism on the southern population. He identified several reasons for the movement of black people to the North, particularly those who had skills:

Race prejudice in the South 1) does not recognize the value of an intelligent, contented laboring class; 2) closes the door to occupations requiring skill and responsibility; 3) drives out of the South, by humiliating and oppressive laws and practices, many of its most desirable citizens; 4) forces across the line thousands of mixed-blood [reference to people of color passing for white]; 5) forces into the ranks of unskilled labor in the North and West many who are skilled.[4]

In light of the experiences of racism along with migration from the South, African American culture served to construct black cultural territory and strengthened a sense of identity. Black migration patterns did not destroy segregation despite hopes, as Bulkley argued, that race relations would be better in the North. A sense of black identity served to combat dehumanization, returning to the idea of resistance culture. Black folk healing was part of this sense of identity.

Ms. Essie remembers her childhood and the ways that healing happened in her family and community in the South. Not just information but also a mindset about health was clearly passed from older generations:

My grandmother was one of those people who could go out in the woods and get anything and cure you. We didn't know anything about no doctors, all they had down there was horse doctors [and] they didn't know nothing but pulling a tooth. They just get those pliers and pull your teeth out and that's it. But my grandma, honey, she know what to do.[5]

Folk healing practices indicated beliefs about the origin and course of various diseases. Ms. Essie's belief about the treatment for measles is one example. "All this talking about giving shots for measles and all this kind of stuff. Shoot, my grandma go out there and get some kind of stuff and make tea out of it, and put us in the bed. . . . Break out every place on your body."[6] In this short statement, she expresses ideas that measles are a type of virus that must "break out" during bed rest as a way to come fully out of the body and result in a cure.

Ms. Essie recalled other cures that were used. Betsy bugs, found beneath rotten logs, were crushed and the resulting liquid dropped in the ear to get rid of an earache. Soot from the fireplace was used to stop bleeding from a cut. Goose grease or tallow was used for chest congestion from colds. She gave an example of treating a fever: "Charles was playing basketball one Sunday and he come in and he had a real hot fever. [We used a mixture of] red onions and Vicks salve and . . . made a poultice out of it and put it on him."

Folk healing was a practical expression of resistance culture, brought from the South to the North, and used to deal with everyday problems. Resistance culture, in this instance, was not some form of political defiance but was tied to the efforts to survive and thrive in the face of seemingly insurmountable odds. Like Ms. Essie and her husband's "get away money," folk healing has helped to set positive boundaries around black people's abilities to care for the self. Ms. Essie's story is not exceptional but indicates beliefs held more commonly among African Americans. The Folk Archives at Wayne State University (WSU) in Detroit were collected in the early 1970s and are a rich source of primary information about black people's healing practices and beliefs.

Detroit Stories

The data in the WSU Folk Archive covers a range of information about Detroiters. Collections of African American folk healing practices are one small part of the whole. Here I draw from twenty-four accounts, gathered by two black and one white graduate student researchers. That the entire interviews were transcribed or preserved on tape, including the interviewers' questions, made relationships clearer than those having to do with the Slave Narratives. To illustrate: the white interviewer floundered: "What I'm trying to understand is, is the peach leaf or the sardine oil going to cure you or does it have to be coupled with a belief in God?"[7] "Why do they work? For example, why does the turpentine cure worms or cobwebs stop bleeding?"[8] The interviewer often asked for an explanation of folk healing that could be compared to the prescriptions of biomedicine. But the relationships of the black interviewers with the folk healing information was different; one, for example, said that she had used some of the remedies herself and "they always seemed to work."[9] The forty or so years' difference between the WSU Archives and the Slave Narratives saw important social changes, including civil rights protests and race rebellions. Mainline research about black Americans no longer had an agenda of supporting white misconceptions.

Most of those who were interviewed in Detroit stated they were from the South, sometimes naming specific towns in Tennessee, Georgia, West Virginia, South Carolina, Mississippi, Louisiana, and Alabama. It was clear that the "South" was a place-marker. Much of the archived material was in the form of transcriptions of tapes; in some cases, the actual tape of the interview was the only record. Some of the archived information was gathered by questionnaire sent to residents of Uniontown, Alabama, where one interviewer's families lived. All accounts cited below were collected between November 1970 and March 1971. These Detroit stories provide more details that resonate with and give greater context to Ms. Essie's stories.

Just as Ms. Essie remembered her grandmother, several respondents identified sources from whom information about folk healing was transmitted to them. One respondent, Mrs. Howell, reminisced, "I was a nosy little girl, and would take after my mother and watch her." But her family was not alone in these practices: "Most families used home remedies of some sort."[10] Another interviewee, Mrs. Kelly, also talked about her family as source of information:

Well, my father was something like an old root doctor. You would call and he used to burn shoe soles and sweet gum balls and things and make up different medications and I would watch him. . . . My grandmother always had me following her through the woods looking for different berries and grasses and things, so I learned a lot from her too, because she lived to be 91 years old.[11]

A few of the informants identified Native American family members from whom knowledge of folk medicines was received. One woman told of practices learned in 1910 from her great grandmother, who was Cherokee.[12] Another identified one of her sources as her grandmother, who was "half Indian, is from West Virginia, and worked for a doctor for awhile."[13] Native American and African American dialogues about healing began as an exchange forced by enslavement. Indians were used as slave labor early in the American colonies. During this time, both African and indigenous slaves were given the same shelters, sometimes mating and producing children. The children of African-indigenous pairings were designated *mustees* in the slave owners' records. Some Native peoples, such as members of the Cherokee, themselves participated in the institution of slavery by owning slaves. Sometimes enslaved Africans joined with native peoples, such as the Seminole, whose villages became safe harbors for escaped slaves. The cultural exchanges between blacks and Indians have resulted in many African Americans claiming Native American ancestry. The relationships between African and Native Americans have become part of a black knowledge base. One of the WSU Folk Archives interviewers, for instance, wrote, "Some elements of [Black Folk Medicine] were borrowed from Indian cultures."[14]

Some respondents discussed folk healing practices within the wider black community's consciousness, more than within the confines of families. One man related how he had learned about folk cures: "You grow up with them, you can't help but know them when you start off on them." [15] One man reported receiving information about a particular cure from a "lady on a bus"; another mentioned a friend as the source of some practices.[16] These comments indicate that there was no secretiveness about healing practices within black communities.

Information was shared and part of a communal knowledge base that was reinforced by the social marginalization of black people. At the same time a hidden interracial text was being written. Some black healing practices were secreted into white Americans' lives.[17]

The Reverend Carter gave an example of the white use of black folk healing. Carter was born in Farmerville, Louisiana, in 1933 and remembered when the healer could come through the town, which had no black doctors and maintained strict racial segregation. Carter recalled that white people, in that very segregated town would "slip" in to see the black doctor. And that white men would "slip" their wives in, where an ironing board was used as an examination table.[18]

The interviewers also collected information about the cures themselves, which were often plant-based. The use of plants highlights another difference between northern and southern living. Within the southern rural lifestyle, there was a clear sense of which plants to use for which cures. Moving to the North altered access to plants and to farming life, and therefore to cures. Awareness of those differences was part of some respondents' discussions. Mrs. Brantley stated: "You see, certain roots and certain things grow in certain places, where something might grow down South, weeds and roots and so forth, they won't grow in Northern states."[19] But there were still possibilities: she asserted one could substitute what did grow there. Other roots could be found: "They grow, you see, because most people see a bunch of weeds, old bushes or something that's unsightly or something and usually just destroy [it]."[20]

Obtaining the correct roots in the North required planning. The Reverend Carter discussed some of the ways that roots for healing work were brought to the area:

> I understand most roots here in the city come from Canada. But most of them I seen people go down south and get them back. Because up here even the trees are different and now you have to be very careful because roots can be very harmful to you. You get the wrong root, you get the wrong thing.[21]

A few pages within the WSU Folk Archives helpfully list folk names with their corresponding botanical names. For instance, turpentine, resin, buds, or needles refer to pine (*Pinus Palustris*) "[a]s tonic, tea, for 'general debility?' chest colds, flue, skin rashes, pinworms." Pork salad is *Phytolacca Americana,* and the leaves are used to make a bath for rashes, chicken pox, or smallpox.[22]

The interviews indicate some of the shifts within patterns of black folk medicine usage, particularly moving from the South to the North. Mrs. Georgia Mae Howell explained how a remedy was transmitted, and how she altered it:

> Well, one remedy that I found I had to—was when I first had my baby. And my breast swole so big with the milk that comes out that I couldn't control it at all. Someone told me about going to get a breast pump and my husband did. But even pumping the milk out wouldn't bring it down. So my aunt Elizabeth came up to see me and she let me know that camphorated oil worked, to rub my breasts with that, and that would help dry the milk up. And when you pump the milk out, take it out and throw it on a hot brick on the fireplace. Well at that time I didn't have a fireplace so I had to throw the milk in a heater. Well I had to reduce that remedy because it worked too good and it really dried me up, and I wanted to feed my baby.[23]

Mrs. Howell had a pragmatic need to control her milk flow. The remedy makes use of a natural element—the oil—with the ritual action of throwing expressed milk on a fire. Her aunt came from the South to transmit this information; Mrs. Howell altered the remedy as needed. In this one account, a given treatment is flexible even as it travels from one region to another. The account demonstrates that folk healing practices interact with related beliefs.

Practices and Beliefs

The stories from different interviews in the WSU Folk Archives portray different ways that folk healing practices were carried out. Mr. Bryce was a child visiting his grandmother in the South at the time of this story he told in December 1970.

> Once I was playing with a knife, and I cut a big gap in my leg. And instead of rushing me to the hospital, like they do today, she [grandmother] took me to her bedroom where she had a fireplace. She reached into the fireplace and got some soot. She went outside and got some spider webs and put that on top of the soot. Then she put a bandage over the whole thing. She told me that this is what they

used to do a long time ago. It healed pretty good, it healed quickly. I didn't feel any pain. I did go to the doctor and he told me I could have been poisoned by this, something that didn't happen.[24]

Some practices were intended to prevent illness. In December 1970, Mrs. Grier gave an example. "My grandmother used to tie asafetida bags around our necks on a little string to keep us from catching colds. And as long as I had my little bag of asafetida on, I never got sick. And one day, my string broke and the next week I had a cold . . . I don't know how [the bag] works, it smells so bad it could fight off any thing."[25] Other cures provided relief for specific conditions. Mrs. Baker told about relief available for menopause. "When they see a woman who, you know, nervous and she's middle age, they'll say right away she must be going through the change and so she's supposed to drink a lot of goat's milk everyday. And this supposed to take away, you know, where she won't be nervous."[26]

Some of the instructions for the remedies were very specific, with certain things needing to be done in ritualistic ways. Mrs. Howell told of the explicit instructions she followed in order to cure fevers in November 1970. "I've had to let the turpentine hit the pulse—you don't rub turpentine on the pulse, you just let it hit the pulse—then put some in a dish under the bed, that would draw the fever right out . . . the turpentine draws the fever away from the body."[27]

These cures had pragmatic purposes. They spoke to creativity in life and the processes of hybridity; shifts from South to North or rural to urban; and finding answers between institutional medicine and home practices. The realities of living, including physical, emotional, and economic health, required thinking in alternative ways. Mrs. Brantley described one aspect of the process: "You need more than you got to survive. So you usually, you know, resort to some other method. This is where gambling comes in, and cooking Southern dinners and other little small items that you want to have for your house that you know you're capable of doing, you can do, just like sewing for others, and washing, taking in laundry, and because it's necessary."[28]

Remedies and cures were used for a range of purposes, not just the physical, such as controlling situations with other people:

Roots are used for, like keepin' evil things away from your door. Your mother-in-law might come in and when she comes in everything goes chaotic, you know. She might upset the whole house and applecart. Now if you want to get her out you have to get a little root and your mother-in-law will maybe get the urge not to come and visit you so frequently.[29]

The distinction between roots and herbs was stressed in this interview. Herbs are medicinal, used for physical cures. Roots are used for other types of works, like keeping your mother-in-law away. Managing day-to-day relationships was part of the wider use of folk healing for spiritual purposes or treating unnatural illnesses. These different uses were known among black community members.

One woman asserted that, in her lifetime, she could see the results of folk healing practices in special ways:

I'm from the South and looking at my relatives and seeing what Black Magic or Voodoo how whatever you want to name it can do to you and others, such as my aunt, she had snakes in her chest now and finding out how they got there and how to get rid of them, now this is something that a medical doctor would like to know.[30]

Reverend Carter, in his 1971 interview, outlined the origin of the remedies that depend on God's guidance:

[The remedies] go back to slave history, way back. They came up with the spiritual means through visions of God. . . . God meant for his people to survive. . . . The only thing they had was to pray to God for wisdom. They couldn't read or write. They wasn't educated so the only thing they had was faith and through faith and prayer God would speak to the mind of people. And he will reveal things to them through visions and dreams. . . . I've seen times I've been sick and my mother prayed and prayed until the spirit told her what to do. . . . This is the same way with the slaves. They always had someone who was close to God in the tribe and God revealed to him what to do. . . . He's smarter than other people and more religious and they go and get him and bring him here. I think in Africa they called him the medicine man, witch doctor. Now, this isn't witchcraft that I'm talking about. It's healing. Now, down home everyone was related to them because they were smart people. So we called them aunt or uncle. This is the honor they give him and when they get

there they look at you like a doctor. No sooner did they look at you
they could tell you right away and tell you what you got.[31]

Reverend Carter's mixture of history and religion demonstrates
cultural hybridity. He inserts a Christian God who is concerned about
enslaved Africans, and who communicates to them in dreams. Then
the cures become a sign of God's favor. Reverend Carter separates the
cures from any relationship to witchcraft. The cures are clearly named
"healing," but there is also a spiritual dimension to his understanding
of healing. The concept of hybridity in black folk healing will be discussed at greater length in chapter 4.

The many cures listed in the WSU Folk Archives, for the most
part, were pragmatic, advising what to do for a sore throat, fever, leg
cramps, or other physical conditions. Some of these cures are practical:
rubbing out leg cramps with oil. Some of the cures seem extreme, such
as one cure for snakebite that advises killing a black chicken and placing it around the bite. A preventive for pneumonia advises wearing
red flannel next to the body. A cure for a baby cutting teeth is to have
the baby wear nine pearl buttons around the neck.[32]

These cures are evidence of different ways of understanding the
relationships of humans with nature (the use of a particular kind of
chicken), what can protect the individual (red flannel), or how biological processes (teething) can be assisted. Each cure expresses a belief in
the interconnections of nature and humans. A human's ability to orchestrate these natural powers conjures healing. None of these healings are fantastic or superstitious to the practitioners but have been
proven over time. The use of the black chicken is reminiscent of African traditional religions, wherein certain animals had the potential to
remove a given evil. The red flannel is reminiscent of hoodoo, wherein
both flannel and the color red were seen as powerful. The teething
button necklace functions as a fetish does, in this case, as an object believed to have power to draw out pain.

Healers in black communities were generally respected, according
to the interviewees. There was knowledge of those people who served
as healers for the community. Mrs. Brantley identified herself a healer
during her interview. She had great confidence in herself and her
methods, saying that she didn't believe in asking preachers for advice
on healing, although she might ask a pharmacist.

> I believe in [my cures] and the modern medicine man believes in his. He believes that penicillin can cure infection which it has done, but if you think back where he got this penicillin, it goes back to the same thing. . . . I believe in God, I believe in [myself] too, so that's all. Between the two of us working together for the same purpose, the purpose will be achieved.[33]

Reverend Carter expressed the importance of the healers in the southern community where he grew up and mentions one:

> He was what they call a two-headed man. . . . Allow me to say he was a doctor in healing. He didn't do no cutting nor giving of shots. . . . They could go out and take a certain tree, a peach tree or apple tree or go out and dig some herbs and boil it and heal you. The same thing you're taking now in medicine in drug stores.[34]

The perceived efficacy of the cures is repeatedly highlighted in these interviews. The belief in the power of the cures contributed to their continuation through the twentieth century.

As discussed in the previous chapter, the majority of African Americans had little or no access to the developing institutionalized medical practice for most of the twentieth century. When such medical care was available, it was dangerous because of the license taken with black bodies. One example of the danger institutional health care posed to black people was sterilization programs. Programs that sterilized African Americans, without their knowledge, to end reproduction under the racial purity ideologies of eugenics grew during and after World War II, particularly in the South. But these incidents were neither as widespread nor as systematic as would occur later.

> During the 1970s sterilization became the most rapidly growing form of birth control in the United States, rising from 200,000 cases in 1970 to over 700,000 in 1980. It is common belief among Blacks in the South that Black women were routinely sterilized without their informed consent and for no valid medical reason. Teaching hospitals performed unnecessary hysterectomies on poor Black women as practice for their medical residents. This sort of abuse was so widespread in the South at these operations came to be known as "Mississippi appendectomies."[35]

These experiences among others did nothing to encourage black Americans to go to hospitals and everything to increase suspicion of institutional medicine. They also added validity to the folk practices. Folk healers were realistic and commendable options to this system of medical abuse.

Ms. Essie had mentioned a cure of red onions and Vicks rub for a fever. She continued:

> When they called the doctor, the doctor come and said "What y'all call me down here for? Y'all done cured the boy already and you didn't need me to come down here." Yeah, they say red onions and that Vicks salve ain't good for you. That's because they want to make the money off of it. They give it a different name, put it in the market, and say it's something else.

As Ms. Essie's comments indicate, there is belief in the efficacy of these remedies. Moreover, some contend that pharmaceutical companies have stolen ideas from traditional healing practices and use the ideas for their own profit. These themes—efficacy and the piracy of black healing practices—are reiterated throughout the accounts from the WSU Folk Archives. These two ideas also bring African American folk healing into direct conflict with institutional medicine.

Black Folk Healing and Institutional Medicine

The interviews from the WSU Folk Archives highlight several indications of sources of tension between African Americans and institutional medicine. Unrecognized contributions of black folk healers to institutional medicine lay part of the groundwork for distrust of institutional medicine. Distrust is evidenced in statements from respondents, such as the already-mentioned comment that herbal cures are "the same thing you're taking now in medicines from drug stores." People who were born in the early part of the century, who already had many reasons not to trust white people, often believed that there were some things institutional doctors just could not do, indicating a general lack of trust. One woman commented that it "was really the older people, they didn't have the hospitals and things. Even some of the older doctors used some of the herb remedies then." In December 1970, Mrs. Armstrong remarked,

> I was reared in the country on a farm. . . . And we never went to a doctor. So if we ever stepped on a nail, my mother used—we call it salt pork now—and she would use it with turpentine. . . . Back then, we didn't believe in doctors, there weren't too many. And anything the doctor could do, they [folk healers] could do better. . . . Doctors have their methods and they give it a big name, but it's just something ordinary.[36]

Additionally, institutional doctors did not know how to effect a cure for someone with an unnatural illness, who had been fixed. Mrs. Brantley, the healer, explained:

> And sometimes when a person that has been hexed or jinxed or however the term might be, well, he might go to a medical doctor, but he doesn't know a thing, then the doctor when he see this, he's unaware of what has occurred to the patient and he has no cure for it. . . . [Folk healers] are the only people that can do it [heal]. A medical doctor, you know, they can do him in.[37]

Mrs. Brantley presented a philosophy behind the differences in folk remedies and institutional medicine, recognizing mystery, emotion, and the ability to see possibilities in the small moments of everyday life.

> There's hidden components in these things, which are unknown to modern medicine, because modern man is so vast in his knowledge that he has looked over small trivial things, which are the most important things, such as the feelings of others. And he has just completely overlooked them because he is highly educated and advanced in everything and money-wise it's good for him; still little small minor things, such as the soot from a chimney, you know, he's looked over these and he wouldn't dream of using soot, getting it all over his clothes.[38]

She discussed the practical dimensions of living under segregation and trying to obtain the emergency services of a medical doctor in the South through most of the twentieth century. "You know, some ambulances didn't used to carry colored people, you had to wait until the colored ambulance come, and get the colored people. Even if the ambulance company was about two miles away, you see, it would only just carry Caucasians and you just have to wait."[39] The unavailability of institutional health care for and the inhumanity shown to black people, along with the system's preferences for white people, insured that folk healers were pragmatic and the preferred options in black communities.

Contrasts between folk healing and institutional medicine by African Americans aided the continuation of folk practices. Certainly, the lack of accessibility to the best of institutional medicine for most African Americans throughout most of the twentieth century helped establish folk healing as a component of black resistance culture. African Americans were often excluded from better, rather than haphazard or experimental, care as well as from knowledge of the scientific advances and knowledge of options for service. As a result, they continued to rely on practitioners with whom they were familiar, to whom they had easy access, and who had a proven track record in their community—folk healers. There were other reasons as well for the survival and growth of folk healing.

African American Folk Healing: Reasons for Survival and Growth

Black cultures changed as African Americans came to northern United States environments. New work songs were sung in the North, out of the fields and into the factories. Housing shaped cultures as apartment living in crowded areas further changed relationships with the land and created different material realities. Urban areas also reshaped leisure time activities: bars, juke joints, after-hours clubs, rent parties, and street dances shaped new expressions of music and movement.

What remained constant, in the North and the South, were the social, economic, and political distances between white Americans and black Americans. The racial gulf was forced by law in some states, by practice in others, but was always present in some form. Near the beginning of the twentieth century, anthropologist and author Zora Neale Hurston wrote an essay with an eye to the literature being published in her time, taking the pulse of the America she knew: "I have been amazed by the Anglo-Saxon's lack of curiosity about the internal lives and emotions of the Negroes, and for that matter, any non-Anglo-Saxon peoples within our borders, above the class of unskilled labor."[40] That lack of curiosity kept people of color in a fixed place in the white mind. The marginalization of African Americans is another component in the retention of folk healing.

But marginalization was not a void but a creative space. Anthropologist John Langston Gwaltney in the early 1970s pursued research in a black community for a number of years. After hundreds of individual interviews and seminars, Gwaltney named the element he called "core black culture":

> From these narratives—these analyses of the heavens, nature and humanity—it is evident that black people are building theory on every conceivable level. An internally derived, representative impression of core black culture can serve as an anthropological link between private pain, indigenous communal expression and the national marketplace of issues and ideas. . . . Core black culture is more than ad hoc synchronic adaptive survival. Its values, systems of logic and world view are rooted in a lengthy peasant tradition and clandestine theology.[41]

Gwaltney presents the creative spirit inherent in core black culture. But his idea of a black-peasant-class tradition does not account for cultural exchanges, as does the use of Native American plant lore that becomes integral to core black culture. Because African American culture was not developed in a vacuum, there were many exchanges with other cultures that served as sources. African American cultures had African cognitive orientations but shifted and changed, especially as ideas from other cultures were added. From these developments, a question often arises: "If black culture has multiple cultural components, is it still *black*?" This question holds the expectation that black cultures can be compressed into simple types. Such expectation of simplicity cannot address the diversity within black cultures nor explain how they are constructed. African Americans can use the same flawed logic and reduce blackness into some essentialized type. The issue of "authentic" blackness buys into a stereotyped understanding of black cultures, ignoring the fact that any living culture grows and changes, as do the people. The issue becomes more confusing when recognizing that African Americans also contribute to and participate in an identifiable American culture, as evidenced by jazz or rock and roll music. The general confusion in American society about what is authentically black magnifies the difficulties in analyzing African American cultures and naming how they develop alongside while drawing from other cultures.

"Cultural hybridities" is a more helpful term for analyzing the cross-cultural developments of African American folk healing. This term is not perfect and has its difficulties because it has too often been used to identify the "pure" or "half breed" based on essentialist lines. Here, however, I am using the term as a descriptive to discuss the processes of the cultural shifts that occur in black folk healing.[42]

"Hybridities" is a term more often used today to provide a variety of ways to think about cultural identity and race, outside the essentialist, reductionist categories of past scholarship. For instance, British anthropologist Robert J. C. Young refers to these processes as the cultural politics of hybridity. His work with hybridities as a line of analysis emphasizes that there has long been a need to have language that could discuss "the mechanics of the intricate process of cultural contact, intrusion, fusion and disjunction" even as he stresses that the term itself will be bound to change.[43]

The concept of hybridities helps explain the adaptability of African American folk healing. Adaptability is another reason the practices have survived. In the new urban environments, practices changed. As some of the 1970s Detroit interviewees pointed out, the plant life was different and the ability to get herbs and roots was not what it had been in the South. No longer could people walk in the yard to find the plant life needed for certain cures or fixes. Pharmacists became new suppliers of roots and herbals. One of the WSU Folk Archives respondents was a pharmacist from Louisiana who had studied at Fisk University and Meharry Medical College. He opened his drugstore in Detroit in 1931. Its stock included basic ingredients for cures and fixes: "castor oil, turpentine, simmer leaves, white oak and red oak bark and asafetida."[44]

White pharmacists also began to sell these items. They even began to create the finished product, which came to be called a "curio" in order not to guarantee success or imply scientific testing. "Curio" sales were so common that Carolyn Morrow Long, a preservation specialist at the Smithsonian, refers to the shift as "commodification of tradi-

tional charms" that began with the twentieth century and grew rapidly during the '20s:

> By the 1930s, anything required by the hoodoo worker—roots and
> herbs, black cat bones and other animal parts, graveyard dirt, lode-
> stones, baths, floor wash, oils, perfumes, powders, sprays, incense,
> candles and prefabricated mojo bags—could be easily obtained from
> spiritual stores and mail order companies.[45]

Such stores were an adaptation to old methods, which became another
form of retaining folk healing practices in black communities.

The WSU Archives interviewees repeatedly mentioned the efficacy of a given cure and the pragmatic ability to care for oneself and
family. The ability to care stood in the face of the lack of availability of
institutional doctors; this fact alone could impress community members. Loudell Snow is a medical anthropologist who has recorded lists
of cures and fixes from her years of research. She implies pragmatism
and efficacy in one category—people see the survivors of folk healing
practices. She notes this as one of three reasons for the continuation of
black folk healing. The other two reasons:

> They [cures] are part of a system that is holistic . . . so that the healthy
> individual is seen as possessing an integrated balance of body, mind,
> and spirit. . . . The system also continues to exist because, unlike bio-
> medicine, it is not restricted to dealing with matters of health and
> illness.[46]

The holistic, wider scope of black folk healing that Snow mentions
becomes an important lens through which African Americans can analyze their current life situations and the beginning of a process to
make social change.

So far, we have discussed eight reasons or ways for the continuation of African American folk healing: (1) the social marginalization of
black Americans, which makes access to institutional medicine difficult; (2) cultural hybridity, which incorporates the remedies of other
cultures; (3) racism within institutional medicine, which denies the
humanity of black bodies; (4) adaptation of practices based on the
availability of materials in new environments; (5) the development of
commerce, which aids in making ingredients available if they cannot

be found naturally; (6) pragmatism, which seeks the most direct line to healing; (7) efficacy, which offers a proven track record to those seeking cures; and (8) a holistic approach, which understands the whole person, not just isolated symptoms in line with black cultural conceptualizations of wellness.

One more aspect has aided the continuation of folk healing: social class in African American communities parallels the structures of class in white American communities. Although the dominant society can set the determinants for low-, middle-, and high-class designations in place, the day-to-day realities are very different for a people who have been marginalized within that society. From the nineteenth century onward, many black Americans understood themselves to be a laboring "class" that had been excluded from society. In the early twentieth century, one thinker wrote of the results of what he termed prejudice, and what we today would call structural racism, on workers in the South: "Race prejudice in the South does not recognize the value of an intelligent, contented laboring class [and] closes the door to occupations requiring skill and responsibility."[47] Acceptance within American society, throughout the North and the South, became an important indicator of a higher social class for black Americans in the first half of the twentieth century. Whether termed accommodationist or assimilationist, the "better class of Negroes" worked to uplift the lower classes of black Americans. These "race men and women" often served as the gatekeepers and interpreters standing between segregated American societies sometimes acting as bridges between black and white worlds.

The "uplifting" of African Americans was linked, in the main, to their decisively turning away from black cultural styles and consciously adopting white lifestyles. Black culture was deemed "low" or the absence of real culture. It is no wonder that in the late 1960s and early 1970s, following winning greater access to civil rights for black people in American society, there were a number of government-sponsored programs that sought to reach "culturally disadvantaged" black youth. The programs were not unique to the 1960s but were part of a long history of programs funded through churches and benevolent organizations for the benefit of the lower classes of black people.

Cultural strata particularly become places to view dialogues within black communities about class. Black feminist historian Evelyn Brooks Higginbotham, as an example, considers the history of religious race records that specifically aimed toward black audiences. She points out that at the turn of the nineteenth century, black religious leaders were arguing against culturally specific *black* religious musical forms, such as the ring shout, and calling for a more formal, written hymnody in church life. In general "literature produced by African Americans strove to negate the pejorative racial images prevalent in film, media, art, and scholarly and popular books."[48] But by the 1920s and 1930s, a social swing began in black communities along with the Great Migrations. The migrants moving into northern urban communities, such as the migrants interviewed for the WSU Folk Archives, became a significant consumer population catered to by record companies. Eventually, migrants and the black working class came to be thought of as carriers of "authentic" black culture: "The twentieth century witnessed the ascendancy of the black working class as the oral narrator of modernity."[49]

There were problems in centering working-class culture as that of "real" black people. As mentioned above, black cultures are often viewed as monolithic, with no diversity. This view is not only external but can be internal to black communities as well. African Americans can become critical of anything other black people say and do that appears culturally "white," including language and personal style. The analysis of black cultural forms itself gets stymied by trying to valorize *the* black expression and demonize anything that is not. Although finding the positive in black culture was an important step, the result has too often been an essentialized blackness.

In a parallel analysis, for those African Americans seeking uplift, folk healing was deemed as a component that should be left behind as part of the effort to change black people's social class. Folk healing was one of the sets of practices that upwardly mobile black people would publicly deny for the first half of the twentieth century. Being viewed as "acceptable" by white communities had a direct economic impact: black people who were seen as not upright in their behavior, as not deserving of public benefits, or as not safe to interact with others might not be employed under wage labor structures. If these groups practiced folk healing, it was done quietly—even as pharmacies and spiritual stores sold items necessary for home use. The black middle class became arbiters of cultural uplift, basing their behavior on white upper-middle-class mores and publicly eschewing folk healing, hoodoo, and conjure. However, those rejected forms of black culture were continued among the maligned black lower and working classes. These included folk healing. Social class, the development of culture across class lines, the analysis of black people who had been shaped by racism—all these differences make researching elements of black culture, such as folk healing, difficult to trace.

These differences are not always apparent to scholars, whose research can become muddled when they try to sort out black cultural patterns. Loudell Snow's research was caught up by an inability to analyze what was really happening in black communities. After cataloguing thousands of folk practices, Snow wrote an essay in 1983 entitled "Traditional Health Beliefs and Practices among Lower Class Black Americans."[50] The title alone implies that black folk healing is only a lower-class activity; a deeper analysis of black cultures is missing.

Differences can be seen between the Slave Narratives of the 1930s and the WSU Folk Archives of the 1970s in regard to the social acceptability of folk healing. The tone of the Slave Narratives documented in the voice of the interviewers and transcribers bordered on ridicule. By the time the WSU Archives records were collected, there was respect for the material; one collector freely mentioned her own use of the cures. Such differences point to cultural changes that aided twenty-first-century retentions of black folk healing.

The first eight reasons addressed in this chapter highlight past to present continuations of folk healing, hybridization, and related issues of social class that may illuminate routes for black folkways to continue in this century. The next chapters, the second part of the book, consider African American folk healing forms in the twenty-first century.

PART II

Today's Healing Traditions

Global influences: An African American spiritual supplies and services store in Columbia, SC, includes healing products derived from locations around the world: Goji (the Himalayas); hoodia (African continent); and magosteen (East Asia). Weight control and detoxification are clearly modern health concerns. Juju and demon slaying are services provided by the storeowner. (Photo taken by author.)

4

Healing and Hybridity in the Twenty-First Century

Don't put your pocketbook on the floor; if you do, you will lose
money.

Don't sweep someone across the feet with a broom or there will be
illness. If it happens, the person whose feet were swept should
spit on the broom.

To determine the sex of an unborn baby, drop a pin on the table in
front of the pregnant woman; if the head points toward her, she's
carrying a boy.

If your right hand itches, it means money is coming. Scratch it toward you and thank God.

To lower blood pressure, take some Spanish moss from a tree and put
it into your drink.

—Healing and protective concepts collected by author, 2003–2006

Introduction

Discussions of African American folk healing today take significantly
different twists than did past discussions. There were hints of the differences to come in the interviews of the Wayne State University Folk
Archives. Folk healing reflects black cultural changes born of the civil
rights, feminist, and Black Power movements. Each movement challenged the status quo to remove or lessen the barriers to greater social
dialogue for those who had been completely shut out of full participation in public life. Each changed the landscape of social possibilities
for African Americans, benefiting some and leaving others behind.

Some of the changes in black American culture and social structures are evident in the contrast between the Slave Narratives and the
WSU Folk Archives records. In the latter, black people were able to

take the lead in some aspects of scholarly methods and theories about themselves. Not all of the changes were welcomed or appreciated by the scholars who self-identified as classicists and opted to maintain the dominance of Western European thought as the only legitimate source of knowledge. The several scholarship camps created some tensions that have not yet been resolved. Nevertheless, African Americans today are able to use research in new ways in analyzing their identities. One way has been to read the subtexts or to identify subjugated voices of black people. But what is sometimes confusing to scholars is that these subtexts or voices are hidden in plain sight in black public spaces. New scholarship has begun to analyze what one scholar has called the black counterpublic: "In black public spaces, in black organizations, and through black information networks, African Americans enter into dialogue with one another . . . an everyday talk that helps black people to develop collective definitions of their political interests."[1]

Black bodies continued to be politicized, through images of the media, work and education, and institutional medicine. As we have seen, the reasons for the continuation of African American healing practices into the current day are numerous. The need to resist oppressions was certainly as much for African Americans who lived during the 1970s Folk Archives era as for those who experienced slavery and the Great Migrations. When black people are compared with other groups in American society, no matter the measure, they are usually found to be in the lowest tier of social success. When considering the number of AIDS cases or the numbers in prison populations, for instance, some people blame African Americans for imprudent sex or criminal tendencies rather than recognizing the effect of structural inequalities that impact black lives.

But resisting oppressions cannot be considered the singular motivation for folk healing's continuance. Certainly, although racism is still experienced, black Americans proactively use religio-cultural forms such as folk healing to construct views of life that advance their own humanity. Black views of humanness can simultaneously be more positive and more complex. African American folk healing encompasses these nuances of resistance with construction, and this adds depth and texture to our study.

Folk healing continues to provide a cultural place where African Americans can define health or illness, care for their bodies, and utilize their spiritual concepts of a holistic universe. The healing advisories at the head of this chapter are an indication of the persistence of ideas about self-care that continue to circulate in black folk healing. These ideas do not mean that other forms of medical care are not sought. Black folk healing in the twenty-first century has become an informal space in which to define self. As folk healing focuses on balancing and renewing life, adaptations take place to fit the present. Relationality and the importance of the interconnections in life have become more important. Relearning the past and finding new ways to move into the future become healing themes.

Ann

Ann is an African American healer living in Detroit whom I interviewed in March 2003. In her early fifties, she also is a writer, media consultant, and teacher. She grew up in the Episcopalian faith, but it did not satisfy her spiritual needs. She explored other religious traditions, and the quest led to different forms of spirituality, such as meditation. As part of one exploration, she visited a hypnotist to lead her through a past-life regression. During this session, she found that she had been a healer in Bahia, Brazil:

> This was in the 1500s . . . in my twenties, I was somehow initiated into a group of women who did healing work, but they did energy work in various forms. For instance, if you were having problems with crops they would come and live with you and work on the crops, which meant they had to work on the family. . . . I was a healer so I had to work on people's sickness.

Following this, Ann believed that one purpose in her life was tied to returning to Bahia. She traveled to Bahia to "reunite her soul to the village." After the trip, she came to another understanding: she felt that greater forces had directed her toward healing work today. "It's like the universe said, no Ann, that ain't why we sent you to Bahia."

Some months later, Ann's mother was scheduled for an operation for colon cancer. The surgeons voiced some concern that she would not survive. "I went back to the hospital, they let me in and she was in prep. So I didn't know what to do. I took my hands and I put them over her stomach and I began to rub. I had no clue. She made it out of the operation, but the doctors were amazed. Then I began to say, Well, I wonder did I do anything—or didn't I?"

Because of these experiences, Ann wanted to study energy healing. She found a program, Healing Touch, through the local alternative medicine newspaper and attended one class session.

> At the end of Sunday, Kathy and Kim [the instructors] came up to me and said, "[We] think you should really continue with your healing touch." And I said "Why?" They said, "Because we really think you have a gift." And I said, "Well gee, thanks. That's like telling me that I should just drop everything that I have been doing and become a mechanical engineer. I'm not really interested."

But Ann did continue taking classes: "It just seemed like whenever a class came, there was money available to take the class."

Ann is now a certified energy healer. She describes the feelings of the healing process.

> It's just awesome. . . . You're not using your energy, what you are doing is channeling the energy of the universe that is out there. You are creating, you are like a wire creating this channel that goes in through your hand and you sort of disrupt disharmony in the energy field and sort of repattern it, so that the person comes back into balance. If a human gets nothing more than that, the fact is that most people are so stressed and off centered, they don't even know what centered is. I've had people come in who say there is nothing wrong with them, but [after a healing session] they go "Wow! This is what it is like to be integrated, to be whole, to be centered!" And you go, "Yeah."

Some African Americans reject Ann's offers of a healing touch session because they interpret it as voodoo. "I have had people tell me, 'Oh no, if it's like yoga, then it's the work of the devil. . . .' Some people have been taught that anything other than what they can see and hear, if their pastor didn't say so, then it's the work of the devil. I don't get it, I don't understand."

Ann believes that the current climate of institutional medicine makes the need for practices like healing touch more pressing:

But you don't have fifty dollars for a doctor's visit and a hundred and some odd dollars for a test and the medication and the prescriptions. I think necessity breeds creativity. If everybody had adequate health care, we may not be seeing all of these alternative things come up again. But people do not have health care. And the health care that they do have—"Just kill me now because that shit's worse than the sickness," you know?

Ann understands that what she does is directly related to any form of healing using energy, and that includes the work of African traditional healers. Connecting ideas of energy work to the history of enslaved Africans, she believes that some of the "power" for hoodoo or voodoo was the use of energy by practitioners. "The thing is that you are sending energy, that's what it is, period. The energy is not good, it's not bad, it's just energy. You know, the same stuff that fuels a television set, can set off a bomb. It's still electricity that goes through. That's neutral. It's the intention of the person that affects positively or negatively." The energy in healing work is what makes it effective and connects other forms of alternative healing: "I could heal you, I could work on you, if you are not here. Reiki can do it. Healing Touch can do it. Therapeutic Touch can do it. . . . I concentrate on sending healing energy to the person."

Healers must be clear on who they are and why they are in healing work. "You have to come in with no judgment because then you start blocking stuff. . . . If you are out there and you are not clear on who you are, or what your problems are or are not, and . . . if you are not real centered in what you are doing, you might as well not do the healing."

The mission of the healer is tied to this use of energy and a holistic understanding of the body. Ann explained:

Part of the mission of the energy healer is to get the person to understand that we are not just dealing with the physical. The physical, that's the last thing that happens. If it comes through the layers, it comes through mentally, physically, so if you are thinking, or you got guilt, you can't let go of stuff, you are ashamed, you are whatever, this builds up energy that eventually manifests. Now it's the energy healer who says, "I'm seeing this in your aura, I'm seeing it, I'm feeling it, or I'm sensing it in your field." So you have to figure out what it is that you can do, so that you will not have a recurrence of this, or it won't build up. . . . Because we don't heal the person, we are the catalyst that kind of works the energy to have the person heal because the body has rejuvenating powers itself. So if you've got blocked energy, I'll help you unblock it so that your body can heal itself. The body has this rejuvenating power, but the physical isn't separate from the mental, the mental isn't separate from emotion.

Energy work, Ann went on, encompasses African healing methods. "That was voodoo, that's African religion. And considering the fact that we were the first humans, and they didn't have [medical] doctors around, that we are probably one of the first people to understand energy." She noted that she would like "to study different African religions to begin to see how they use energy."

Contemporary African American Folk Healers

African American folk healing has hybridized from past knowledges and practices. It no longer looks or feels the way it had been represented in the Slave Narratives or even the WSU Folk Archives records. Some aspects appear similar—as do the cures cited at the head of the chapter. All of the opening comments were gathered in passing conversations with African Americans. None of those speakers asserted that he or she had taken the prescribed cure, but the knowledge was simply present in their communities. Most of the statements were collected from black college students.

Ann clearly identifies herself as a healer, yet she appears different, more educated than the people in the 1930s or 1970s. By some views, Ann would be disconnected from past folk healers and dropped into a category of "alternative" healer. Yet she still connects with the black community and sees herself as very much embedded in African American cultural perspectives. That she also has a sense of being connected to her past life demonstrates a sense of connections between living and dead. She has chosen to be a healer but based on her gift and her past life; from this base she sought help to hone her gift. By some other views, Ann should have moved so comfortably into Western cultural mores that her racial identification would be optional, if not completely erased. But that has not been the case for Ann, or for the black college students who were included in the opening quotations.

Ann's decision and the decisions of the middle-class college students to remain connected with ideas of healing and thereby folk healing resonate with a study by psychologist Fayth M. Parks. After having conducted two hundred interviews of mostly middle-class, Christian black Americans, she found that "folk healing beliefs and practices were identified as important coping strategies. I found that traditions were kept alive within families via storytelling."[2] From her survey, Parks also identified four elements that identified and framed African American folk healing for her interviewees: (1) a sense of connection with a spiritual dimension; (2) the use of ritual to connect with the spiritual dimension; (3) belief in the power of words; and (4) the use of dreams as omens of, or providing direction for, the future.[3] These elements also underline the definition of folk healing that is used in this book.

Ann's story demonstrates that forms of folk healing in black communities have taken new shapes. Folk healing is not as it was in the past, when African American communities were isolated enough to retain and pass on folklore practices. Ann's education, gender, and class are factors in the retention and hybridization of folk healing. A look at how events of the mid-twentieth century shaped the current realities is necessary to understand these developments.

Social Changes

The case *Oliver Brown et al. v. Board of Education of Topeka, Shawnee County, Kansas, et al.* (347 U.S. 483, 1954) was more than a simple challenge to the past structures of inequalities in America. The 1954 decision ended a system of segregation that had kept many black men and women in positions that were little more than neoslavery since the 1896 *Plessy v. Ferguson* (163 U.S. 5337, 1896) "separate but equal" decision that reinforced sharecropping, day labor, and domestic work at unequal pay rates. *Brown v. Board of Education,* although focused on one social arena, effectively began dismantling segregation through mandating access to public education.

Although black Americans heralded the *Brown* decision as critically important, using it as a catalyst for further actions in the civil rights movement, it was not well received by white segregationists. Many white students were pulled from public schools and enrolled in private schools. The concentration of black students in U.S. urban schools became an additional factor in precipitating white flight from cities to suburbs and beyond.

Social class structures were built into these educational battles. As African Americans continued to seek education as a way for self and community improvement, many all-black communities became places where lower-quality goods and services, including education, became normative because of high poverty rates. Black Americans have significant populations in twenty-one states but are more heavily concentrated in urban areas such as New York, Los Angeles, and Detroit.

At the same time, black people who are college educated use their education to retain and preserve their cultures and history. Attending college is not a panacea for racial relations. With few exceptions, cultural and racial identification is reinscribed through encounters with white mainstream America. Many college-educated black women and men will blend what they have learned in colleges and universities and in the workplace with their own cultural referents, emphasizing the idea of hybridity. This blending of classroom information with lived experience reconstructs knowledge to fit their lives. Some black people, therefore, help to maintain folk healing as they use their college educations to find ways to preserve their folk cultures.

When I began this research, I was surprised to find the number of women who either pursued healing as a folk art or blended folk ideas into their training from institutional medicine. I had expected a greater balance of men and women in folk healing. Later, I came to understand the importance of embodied spirituality, and the continued impact of race, class, and gender oppressions. The number of women I interviewed and encountered helped me understand the sharp differences between exploring healing from a folk perspective as opposed to studying healing from the perspective of biomedical culture. Institutional medicine relies heavily on male, corporate, and competitive behaviors to control both the healer and the ill person. The work of folk healing, in contrast, is accessible to any who are gifted and able to draw on the spiritual awareness to do so. For African American women, this holistic spirituality has informed most of their lives. The majority of black women still struggle daily with the combined impact of race, class, and gender. But the healer does not depend on an institutional appointment or reward system to feel successful. The person who seeks a healer depends on his or her own intuition and the healer's past record of efficacy as determinants of the healer's capabilities. In the folk healing process, gender does not establish access to power.

African American women have found ways to work around their marginalized status, including use of folk knowledge in the development of new forms of folk healing. Ann's story is one example. Black women's access to ideas of folk healing is due to the continued existence of embodied spirituality. This spirituality may be nurtured at home or in church. African American women's embodied spirituality is more than charismatic expression. Embodied spirituality is grounded in a different perspective of the human person, a perspective that unifies body and soul within the life of the past, present, and future community in conversation with an ever-present God. This holistic view of the person in community is a ready-made construct for development of, or attachment to, folk healing. This holistic view of the human reflects African cognitive orientations, thereby linking black people across the African Diaspora with religio-cultural patterns from the African continent.

Ann's story reflects social changes among African Americans at the same time that it demonstrates connections to African American folk healing traditions of the past. For instance, Ann referred to *energy,* which had no name in past records. The new wording should not be a reason to view Ann as disconnected from the past but rather shows a link between past and present. This connection can be seen in the following two quotations. The first is from an unnamed informant in the Slave Narratives collected in the 1930s:

> The doctor . . . treated her for 'bout two weeks but she didn't get no better. A friend told us to try a root worker. . . . The root worker come that Wednesday mornin' and looked at her, but he never touched her. He told us she had been hurt, but he could have her on her feet in 'bout a week or ten days. He didn't give her no medicine, and he

never come back 'til she was up and walkin' 'round. She got up in 'bout seven days, and started talkin' earlier than that.[4]

Ann provides the second quotation:

> Anybody who does this healing work can come through a medical standpoint or a religious standpoint. I tend to feel that it is more of a religious standpoint for me—not a religious but a spiritual thing. Because how does this work? Because I may touch you . . . and I might not even touch you. How is it that you are feeling better? . . . It's the energy, because you are not doing it. It's the energy that you are allowing to move through you and out, into that person's energy.

Both speakers recognized the efficacy of the methods used, which sound remarkably similar, although Ann's understanding of healing incorporates multiple perspectives.

Education and travel become routes for African Americans to journey beyond their immediate community's wisdom sources to find information on healing. International travel is more widely accessible today, and many black Americans choose to travel to the African continent or the Diaspora. At the same time, African emigration to the United States increased significantly throughout the 1990s. Opportunities exist as never before for African Americans to dialogue with, and learn from, Africans. These possibilities add new dynamics and a growing sophistication to African American cultural expressions and analysis. The wider palette of choices may involve reaching outside the knowledge base of the black American community, and then finding ways to reinterpret and bring the knowledge back in. As in the past, creativity is used to blend these various strands—the hybridization process.

Ann was still a student of healing touch when I met and interviewed her. Fully certified now, she intends to open a healing center in Detroit, a majority-black city. Ann's journey took her from Brazil to her mother's hospital room to healing touch classes. Her clientele is significantly African American. A sense of being present to and for the black community permeates Ann's work. This is her intent, despite the clear resistance of some African Americans to participation in such healing.

African American folk healing in the twenty-first century is not lifting past practices of folk healing whole cloth—such as those cited from the 1970s Folk Archives of Wayne State University or excerpts from the Slave Narratives of the 1920s. It is the fine strands, the spirit rather than the letter, that are transferred to contemporary practices. These practices may utilize contemporary knowledge, but practitioners still self-identify themselves and their work as "black." Hybridity is clearly at work. Past ideas and practices are constructed with current concepts. Sokara's story, below, highlights the sets of relationships between past and present practices even more finely.

Sokara

Sokara's story parallels Ann's in some ways with regard to access to educational and international travel options. Sokara is also in her early fifties. Both women's lives overlap the social changes of the 1950s and 1960s. They were growing up in the late 1960s and through the 1970s, the time period of the WSU Folk Archives interviews in chapter 2. Both women's experiences and knowledge bring something new to an understanding of African American folk healing. Sokara's experiences have been more extensive.

Sokara was living in Ohio when I interviewed her in March 2004. Some years ago, she was led to healing work while living in California; at that time, she owned an African art gallery.

> I was having a lot of trouble selling the art. Not trouble attracting clients. But the gallery, "Cultures and Consciousness," became well known. There were pieces I was having a hard time letting go. And part of the reason that I was having a difficult time is that I was having dreams. In the dreams, I would see myself sitting with a client. I had certain masks or other pieces of traditional art from Africa and I was channeling energy through the pieces into the client . . . and when people would come to buy them, I would be really upset.

Sokara felt drawn to study any method to understand what was happening to her. A nearby institute, Three in One Concepts: Mind, Body, Spirit Integrated, offered training in applied kinesiology (applied kinesiology is a form of testing muscles to determine spiritual, mental, or physical disharmony in a person's current or past life). She closed the gallery and concentrated on her studies. She traveled to different locations, including Charlotte, North Carolina, focusing on this healing work for a year. But these were not drastic steps for her. She had had periodic precognitive dreams that she felt gave her visions of the future and she acted on the dream messages. During her teen years, Sokara had studied "spiritual cultivation from different systems." She concentrated on Hinduism particularly because she "remembered a lifetime in India. I was really putting my parents on the spot: Why don't you take me home? They were really good natured about it."

After completing training, Sokara and her seventeen-year-old son traveled to Britain, again directed by dreams. She lived there for two years and became known for working with black mental health using the methods of mind-body integration. "There's all these centers in Britain, in all the boroughs, there are these women's centers, and especially centers devoted to ethnic minority women. And I was being invited to every one of these boroughs to do work, because it was the thing. The U.S. in many ways is far behind in complementary healing and health." She returned to the United States in 1995, but continues to travel and has given workshops in Denmark, Sweden, and India. For African people, Sokara believes that muscle testing can be critical for self-understanding. "I think it can be important for any people, but for us, for African Americans and Caribbeans, because we had had so much trauma that was unspeakable trauma—unspeakable in the sense that we couldn't put our finger on what happened. Why did it happen? When did it happen? Who did it happen to? And how did it happen? And so we were acting out, with things we couldn't identify."

Working with one form of healing led her to learn other forms. "It was kind of like if you speak two, three, or four languages, then five, six, and seven, adding a few on is not a problem. . . . Synthesis seems to be my thing." In addition to mind-body integration, Sokara makes use of Reiki; color therapy; Bach flower essences; gemstones; crystals and crystal elixirs; and innovative vibrational work that uses art related to the ancestors that she has developed. "As a consequence, I call my approach 'the healing tapestry,' talking about weaving threads together, bringing things that seem to be disparate together to create a whole." In spite of all her work, Sokara declares, "It's not easy to be a practitioner in a black body." One reason for the difficulty in practice in the United States is the lack of health care options through the dominance of institutional health care.

I don't do much kinesiology work anymore because here, I don't have access to the people. One of the things that bothers me is that the people who could benefit the most cannot afford to do a session with me because insurance won't pay for it. Or they would take Jack Daniels over the kinesiology session. . . . I have wanted for so long to take one dozen black men and train them in this to work with other black men.

The second problem is that when Sokara has an opportunity to teach the methods, race becomes a factor.

I hate to teach a muscle-testing course to [racially] mixed audiences. Because when I work with all Africans—you can put ten Africans in a room coming from any culture and start working with them. You say the course is going to run from nine to five, it will not. It'll go till the next morning. It will become a spiritual séance, a vision quest. People speak in tongues. They speak ancient languages, off planet. They have experiences that are off the wall. And when white people are in the room, two things happen. Either they become frightened by the power of what's coming through or the Africans start shutting themselves down so they're not fully expressing.

I discussed the distinction between black healing practices and metaphysics with Sokara. She noted the power of healing practices of people of color:

What a lot of white scholars and students of so-called metaphysics are calling "metaphysics" is the retentions of indigenous peoples' work. It's African, Native American, and Asian peoples' work reworked and put into another language. It's culture theft, that's what it is. What people are calling metaphysics was First People's worldview to begin with. Because the cosmology—of the universe, of the earth, the ancestors, the holy cosmic forces—which in Yoruba might be called Orisha or in Akkan would be called by another name. But what they're calling metaphysics is really a way of saying, "You people don't have anything, you're just trying to do a knockoff." It was our work to begin with. And if we don't understand that, and we're not really clear, then people will continue to say, "You're not doing anything."

The Range of African American Folk Healing

Sokara's story highlights that African American folk healing concepts are not limited to a single act or type of activity. Both Sokara's and Ann's stories introduce a variety of ways that African American folk healing is diffused through black experiences today. Both women bring a mindset to their studies and work that is informed by their cultural perspectives, that indicates an epistemology that is different from the biomedical culture. Neither woman felt detached from the realities of being black in the United States because they had studied healing outside black communities. Although Sokara had more clearly defined it, both women understood what they did in context of being black.

Sokara's experiences define her healing work as clearly out of the countryside, into urban settings, and grounded in global events. She explores the world as part of her healing work. This fearless exploration is clear in the ways she mentioned being influenced by multiple religious traditions beyond Christian. The innovative healing method that she has developed came from her connections with, and explorations of, African religions. Part of her aim, in the new method, is to tie into African ancestral work in ways that will not frustrate or put off the person seeking healing; like Ann, Sokara recognizes that African forms of spirituality are frightening to some African Americans. Therefore, she uses art to assist healing processes, such as

> [a]llowing the ancestors' voice to come through you in [your] writing, to get in touch with the major themes in your life. . . . You know, if I say, we're going to put candles and glasses of water out, we're going to have an animal sacrifice, and that we're then going to call on these deities, that's very off-putting for a lot of people. . . . To many people who've been trained in Christianity, that just would not be acceptable, it would be frightening, some of the ways that traditional African process would go. But this art process is much easier for people to access. To say we're going to work with art and to work with

our emotional content and work with how the body is genetically carrying the message of the ancestors is much more palatable for people. . . . [T]hat is part of the continuation of the ancestral river.

Sokara and Ann both indicated awareness of their gifts and talents, and actively sought ways to obtain the help they needed to follow their paths to healing work. Both women have found creative ways to utilize their training, following uncharted directions. Both are in the business of healing. Because they are businesswomen, they utilize marketing and business practices to draw clientele.

Folk healing among African Americans has always been more than herbs and roots. Black people apply creativity in defining their bodies along with their relationships to the community and the cosmos. Spiritual survival is set in motion with this approach. Contemporary African American folk healing may integrate ideas but will retain some sense of black cultural resistance against the dominant American culture.

As we have seen, African American folk healing is relational, aiming for rightness in how humans relate to each other and one another. Relationships, whether between husband and wife or parent and child, are understood as areas that can be healed. Beyond the immediate family, the local or global community may be in need of healing. Healing is possible on many levels, even beyond the human world. Such a view of healing indicates the sense of being in relationship: with human, plant, animal, or spirit life. Being in relationship includes natural elements, such as water, and specific animals. Spirits of the deceased are part of this relational world and another place where healing may be needed. Divine beings are intimately part of this cosmos able to interact, to offer healing, or to be in relationship that needs healing. These are African-derived perspectives with an interdependent view of life, understanding interconnections between all beings.

All of these components are sources of power or ill fortune, depending on the practitioner. These understandings of relationality are indicative of a spirituality that defines the cosmos and the Divine in a framework that is aligned with some African conceptualizations. African American folk healing revolves around this sense of rightness: healing is understood as making something or someone "right." The definition of what is *right* will depend on the persons involved. This concept is applied in various ways. For example, an African American medical doctor told me that she believes that healing is not possible unless the person who is ill has the *right* mindset, is willing to be healed. She will not perform surgery if that mindset is not present in her patients. I asked her if she learned this in medical school, and she laughed and replied that she had not. Where does this kind of interpretation originate if not in medical school? Is it only her experience? What factors indicate a "right mindset"? These questions point to the importance of intuition in making choices: there are no set scientific indicators, but the "feel" of a situation becomes a determining factor.

With these ideas of African American folk healing, another critical aspect is brought to light. Black theologian Dwight Hopkins has presented the conjurer, which he describes as one who "works with *nature* to manipulate the spiritual powers *of all creation* for human advancement."[5] The conjurer, Hopkins contends, is an archetype. The distinctive category presents new ways of thinking about folk healing, not only in the various forms by which it is practiced but, most important, for the mythic value within African American communities. The conjurer can heal or harm but Hopkins identifies the deepest meaning as informing spirituality: "To be human, in the fullest sense imaginable, derives from attending to the gifts of nature or of all creation."[6]

Another understanding of the importance of the healing and conjuring figure in black communities is laid out by black feminist religious historian Yvonne Chireau as she explores hoodoo:

> African American magic is all around us. It resonates in contemporary manifestations of Hoodoo, in the ritual creations of African diasporic religions, and in the vibrant artistic forms that utilize conjuring themes. Even as numerous black American supernatural traditions are fully alive in the twenty-first century, their sources are not readily apparent. Theirs is not a pure, unmediated connection to an essentialized African origin, but a hybridized lineage, one that is additive, constantly recreated, and shaped according to circumstance.[7]

Hopkins's and Chireau's analyses bring me to ask: Is African American folk healing a component of a black mystical tradition? Exploring the answers to this question delineates another dimension of African American folk healing.

A Black Mystical Tradition and Folk Healing

Some mystical traditions are influenced by the idea of hermits who withdrew from the world to pray and meditate to become closer to God. At times, ascetic practices are used to aid in the focus on the Divine. Some of these mystical traditions also consider the spiritual dimension as the higher and more important dimension of the human person.

I am defining a mystical tradition as a tradition that aids the believers to experience the self as timeless and unbound, in order to transcend the present. Reaching for this transcendence aims to comprehend the Divine better. In many traditions, the purpose of the mystical activities is to become more fully involved in life; for some, this mystical road leads to work for social justice.

An African American holistic view of life, with possibilities for the human person to connect with the supernatural, clearly falls within this broad view of a mystical tradition. I do not mean here a sense of the mystical that removes itself from everyday life but one that becomes more deeply immersed in exploring other humans and nature. The aim of such mystical immersion is to become a more fully human, and therefore more fully spiritual, being in community. The cognitive orientations brought from Africa have been influenced by contemporary exchanges among communities within the African Diaspora. In this frame of thinking, art is within life and its experiences, not to be enclosed in museums. Living is itself an art. Full engagement with the community is meditative. Divinity could speak through nature as well as other people and community events. All life can be understood as a daily meditation. In these understandings, black Americans bring a spirituality that is clearly influenced by African ideas.

A story from Sokara emphasizes these points. She was working in London using kinesiology techniques with a black man who had anger issues:

> And so here I am with this man, muscle testing him, and we're talking about his daughter and we're working on his rage. . . . all of a sudden he jerked his arms up like that [demonstrates] like there were chains on them and he was vibrating. . . . and tears were rolling down his face. . . . And I called out to him, "Where are you?" "I'm in

a hole in the ground, I'm in a hole!" "Where are you?" "I'm in Mali!" I said, "What is going on?" He said, "We have been taken from the village, we are in a pit, they are taking us from our families." And he cried and cried and cried. And talked about the loss of his family. And then he started talking about the loss of his daughter. Then I started working on his heart chakra, and telling him to just release his grief. And just let it go. I know that he was not going to get through that whole piece in an hour or two. And then I had him do some work on grieving and bringing him back out of that. . . . [When the session was through], I sat in front of him and put my hands on his knees and said, "Do you understand what has happened? Do you understand your rage?" And he said, "Yes." . . .

Sokara uses different modalities (kinesiology, past-life regression, and chakra healing) to deal with a man's unresolved anger from a being enslaved in order to effect healing in his emotional life now. This is mystical transcendence.

One author draws from African understandings to delineate the idea of transformation based on ordinary objects:

Pots and hoes are emblems of knowledge of how to carry out acts of transformation—magical or medicinal acts—and pots in particular are legendary objects admittedly instrumental to religious worship. . . . Knowledge of how to use pots and hoes as tools of transformation is within some communities sacred information, for it is knowledge of how to pray, and thus a form of medicine in the traditional sense.[8]

In such a view, the mystical happens within life, and prayer is not divorced from action. A life is well lived by generating more life and wisdom for the good of the community. Understanding that all life is connected, including the Divine, nature, the past, and the future, means that dreams are sources of communication. This was seen in Sokara's story wherein she made life decisions based on precognitive dreams. In this understanding, dreams are ways that an ancestor sends a warning or God provides direction. In Fayth Parks's survey, mentioned earlier, the four elements of folk healing uncovered were spirituality; ritual; belief in the power of words over personal well-being; and belief in dreams, signs, and omens.[9] Each of these is a reference to the mystical, to the belief in a holistic view with power that is accessible, and to communication with the Divine.

To think of folk healing in this mystical framework clearly takes it out the realm of cultural quirks and confirms the need for the widest definition that can encompass the many healing activities in African American life and thought. Cures are possible because of power within items or within the healer. One of the respondents from the 1970s WSU Folk Archives stated, "Everybody else believes because everybody else is still practicing, practicing now in this day and age. This is the age of modern science and modern miracles. But the old remedies shall remain."[10]

Black Culture, Hybridity, and Folk Healing

Race, cultures, and black bodies indicate several sets of relationships that continue to play a role in shaping contemporary black folk healing in the United States. These are different from historic relationships, from those as close as fifty years ago. The changed relationships are organically related to those from the past but reflective of the changing times. Similarities between past and present black cultural practices are found in the continued African cognitive orientations, even though they may be expressed in different forms across history. There are similarities in the processes of using black experience as the perspective and the point of departure for cultural developments. There are strong similarities in situations that retain black Americans in separate spaces: practices that materially create different spheres of influence for sets of Americans separated by race will always produce disparate cultural influences.

But there are significant differences that add points of stress to a study of African American folk healing. So far, the slipperiness of the idea of black culture is more evident in this chapter. *Black* culture is tied to a racial construct. *Who* is black is not always clear, especially as more people designate their own racial categories on governmental forms, categories such as "biracial" or "other." There is some benefit to this, as one author states: "One recognizes that people are not simply racial objects (to be verified from without) but racial subjects with an interiority that is never completely and unquestionably clear."[11]

The first chapters of this book focused more on history and had a clearer view of what was or wasn't black or black culture that was significantly an inheritance of a sharply segregated America. But, with Ann's and Sokara's stories opening our discussions of present-day folk healing, the lines are no longer sharply drawn. Sociologist Tommie Shelby emphasizes this view:

> The imperative to conform to black culture would require individual blacks to possess the capacity to identify, if only implicitly and roughly, which elements are components of their culture and which are not. The problem is that there is no consensus on just what characteristics these are or on how they are to be distinguished from elements of white culture. In fact, what is culturally black is one of the most contested issues within the greater black population.[12]

However, enduring racial tensions within U.S. society continue to construct a location where black Americans self-identify as being black, despite all other social changes. Shelby also points out that fighting against racism and its effects becomes a collective struggle that is "a cherished inheritance for many black Americans."[13] This collective struggle is also a matter of consideration for African American folk healing, as will be seen in the following chapter.

The difficulties of defining who is black, along with the changing dimensions of black culture, highlight the importance of using the term "hybridity," as discussed in the previous chapter, to address the ways African American folk healing changes over time and in conversations with other cultural groups. At the same time, African American folk healing, despite the slipperiness of racial and cultural definitions, is one category that still retains a clear black culture label. The processes of hybridity definitely aid in the retention of the black culture label early into this twenty-first century. The photo at the beginning of this chapter presents a visual of the hybridized category of black culture in the realm of healing. The store is named "Sphinx Paw," drawing on Egyptian imagery, stressing the sense of connection to the African continent. But the product lines are drawn from a global array: hoodia from Africa; magosteen from East Asia; and goji from the Himalayas. All of these are mixed with available healing services: juju or demon slaying.

Processes of hybridity simultaneously diffuse folk healing into American culture. These exchanges across race and culture lines, on one hand, make this study of folk healing or any other aspects of black culture difficult to capture neatly. On the other hand, these exchanges can be enlivening because they demonstrate the rich complexity of human beings.

Maafa event in New Orleans, July 2004. (Photo taken by author.)

5

Healing the Past in the Present

The young woman explained to me how to protect an accident-prone loved one. Take a small mirror into which no one else has looked. Hold it so that the person to be protected looks at his or her own reflection. Place the mirror under a living plant—houseplants work best. Water and care for the plant, thereby protecting the loved one. Of course, the same process can be used to cause harm by breaking the mirror into pieces, and also placing that under a plant.

—As told to author, July 2005

Introduction

The previous chapter situated African American folk healing in the twenty-first century as a continuation of past practices and concepts hybridized by education, class, gender, and contact with Africans through the Diaspora. Two modern-day black women's stories emphasized how folk healing retentions are woven into the lives of some black Americans. Folk healing, for many African Americans, offers remedies including herbal cures and ritual performances to address the evil of the past and foster something new. These conceptions of healing emerge from African American culture. They operate at archetypal and therefore mythic levels that are not always recognizable as stemming from folk traditions. Beginning with a look at folk healing in light of black intellectual traditions, this chapter focuses on four ways that such healing is manifested by African Americans to heal social ills: names and identity; reparations; connections with the slave past; and an organization that aims to heal.

Black Intellectual Traditions and Folk Healing

Ann's and Sokara's stories emphasize some aspects of the definition of African American folk healing that is outlined at the beginning of this book, such as the overlapping of the past into the present; a focus on ancestors; and the use of dreams, words, or actions to access power to make changes.

African American folk healing is defined by a focus on connection with others, nature, the dead and the unborn, and a belief that sickness is caused by more than germs. Healing offers a language through which African Americans dialogue with the world. The range of folk healing practices discussed in previous chapters is soaked into African American consciousness and epistemology. Treating illness and aiming for health entails a scope expanded beyond the limits of the physical self, emphasizing connections to the community and nature and nations, as well as links with the past and future. Healing past errors, social ills, and injustices thus becomes part of the dynamics of black folk healing. As such, healing social ills constitute public expressions of a black mystical tradition as discussed in chapter 3. We saw the work of Sokara, who healed a man's anger over enslavement; the work of healing social ills is in the same vein. Racism and oppression, and their effects can be considered illnesses within a mindset retentive of black folk healing understandings. Because many of these ills are rooted in enslavement and racism, the past must be considered as part of the healing process. Healing on a larger scale than Sokara's work but still with a folk mindset might involve large-scale dreams of what the nation could be to local, creative rituals. The healing will encompass community life, aspects of citizenship, and relations with the U.S. government.

Some might view the combating of social problems with folk remedies as the desperate efforts of powerless people. But drawing on the archetypal images of the conjurer and the interconnections of all reality, African Americans make strong use of myth. Myth fuels the human imagination and provides frames of reference for living. Myth traverses intellectual and emotional areas of human life, informing individuals while shaping communities. Healing society or the past is a viable option from an African American epistemology.

This view of African American folk healing brings it squarely within a black intellectual tradition. Within black thought, the healing is a cohesive partner in the struggle to identify aspects of, and then to address, American history. History is not merely a series of past events that can be noted by scholars but becomes part of black American consciousness. How groups of black people choose to deal with the past will vary from religious responses to social programs. Constructing any response is an intellectual endeavor. The intellectual work may take an artistic form, such as Langston Hughes's mid-twentieth-century poetry that posed the question "What happens to a dream deferred?" The search for an answer was motivation for another artistic work, the prize-winning 1950s drama by Lorraine Hansberry, *A Raisin in the Sun*. The creation of art to explore the human condition is certainly an intellectual task. For African Americans, such art also holds a healing dimension as we find ways to voice the realities of our lives' conditions.

The art used to give expression to black conditions is, first and foremost, healing for African Americans by enhancing the quality of our lives. Black writer and cultural critic Ralph Ellison pointed this out in the 1950s regarding blues music:

> For the blues are not primarily concerned with civil rights or obvious political protest; they are an art form and thus a transcendence of those conditions created within the Negro community by the denial of social justice. As such they are *one of the techniques through which Negroes have survived and kept their courage* during the long period when many whites assumed, as some still assume, they were afraid.[1]

The poet or blues artist functions as healer, conjuring words and emotions to cleanse or strengthen. A brief story will illustrate. On meeting the noted black feminist poet Sonia Sanchez, I surprised myself with my reaction: I threw my arms around her and said, "You saved my life!" Her response to my exuberance was telling: she was not surprised but simply nodded her head. The idea of poetry *saving a life* or the poet's calm acceptance of the declaration indicates an artistic level of communication among African Americans that is both intellectual and healing.

This discussion returns to the perceptions of interconnections among all life that brings art and politics into a communal framework where healing can happen. One author identified what she termed "the African American philosophy of life":

> As in African belief, God is the most senior member of the community and guardian of the community. . . . God is radically in community through the concept of the family and the interrelated circle of God and the ancestors. . . . The community comprises the living and those who are dead. The past generations who are in the spirit world are ancestors of the individual and the individual is linked to all of them. . . . The community is hierarchical from the oldest to the youngest.[2]

Placing these concepts of the connections of life within a *philosophical* framework identifies them as intellectual labor, even if they function in folk ways.

A focus on healing the past emerges from African Americans' undeniably oppressive history. Although most African Americans today have no personal memory of enslavement, family and community members' stories maintain a salient awareness of this history. The Jim Crow years following Emancipation kept oppression at the center of black consciousness. There are both heroic and shameful stories in most black families that keep a sense of the past alive.

Museums of African American history play an important role in facilitating remembering. Efforts to develop and open such museums around the country speak to an awareness of the past and a focus on healing in the present, while looking toward a better future. When I served as a visiting scholar at the Charles H. Wright Museum of African American History in Detroit, I was impressed by how much historical material is held and guarded by folk historians. It was not unusual to find people who had collections such as all the posters from movies produced by African Americans in a given period or every issue of a long-terminated black publication, stored in their basements. To hold on to pieces of the past certifies them as having value. Because they have value, the saved objects also establish the related portion of black lives as important, not to be discarded. This treasuring of the past can be considered part of a process of healing black American experiences of racism and oppression. In African American imaginations, the past structures the present. As a result, the social problems of the current day add to a sense of the need to be healed.

Dreams of Africa and Changing Names

African Americans identities have been shaped by the history of slavery. Following enslavement, black Americans suffered the experience of being citizens in a country that treated them as disposable goods. When African Americans look at their lives, they see the unfulfilled promise of what could be if they were able to fully participate in American society. Still today, shortcomings in education, housing, wealth, and employment are exacerbated by the recognition of the marginalization of black culture and ideas from mainstream America. These realities have shaped a desire to bring about healing for past trauma that has led up to the present. The longing for wholeness has informed aspects of black public life even if there is no agreement on the shape the healing should take. There have been many efforts toward healing. The exploration of black identities is one route that brings relationships with white Americans to the fore.

The continent of Africa continues to hold symbolic meaning for black Americans. At times, the wish to return "home" has offered a fantasy about being in a place where white people's hatred can no longer cause harm and freedom will be found. One symbol of such freedom dreams of Africa is reflected in the stories of High John de Conquer, some of which were collected by Zora Neale Hurston. High John "had come from Africa. He came walking on the waves of sound. Then he took on flesh after he got here. . . . High John de Conquer went back to Africa, but he left his power here, and placed his American dwelling in the root of a certain plant. Possess that root and he can be summoned at any time."[3] Hurston pointed out that High John brought hope and a sense of being protected to a people. To offer hope to a people caught in a system that stripped them of social power and dehumanized them is a radical form of protection. Folk healers could use a root called "High John" to call on nature to protect people from harm. Hurston's account makes clear that the power of this imagery did not end with enslavement. In fact, this root is still used today.

A real or imagined relationship with Africa has continued to be salient for black Americans throughout their history. The prospect of healing black American identity broken from their lands of origin by reconnecting them to a mythologized African past is a possibility that has held black imaginations. This fascination is reflected in song and art as well as politics. The Harlem Renaissance (1919–1940), for

example, initiated a new focus on Africa, such as the poet Countee
Cullen's (1903–1946) "Heritage," which included these lines:

> What is Africa to me:
> Copper sun or scarlet sea,
> Jungle star or jungle track,
> Strong bronzed men, or regal black
> Women from whose loins I sprang
> When the birds of Eden sang?
> *Over three centuries removed*
> *From scenes his fathers loved,*
> *Spicy grove, cinnamon tree,*
> *What is Africa to me? . . .*[4]

Throughout this lengthy poem, Cullen's frustration is clear as he
names ways that the American experience has divorced him from
awareness of his own identity. The loss of identity includes how experiences of Christianity separated him from a spirituality that is not
known but is missed.

A sense of "home" is still connected with the idea of Africa in the
minds of many black people today; the commercial success of African
clothing and decoration gives evidence of these connections. Yet, there
is still distance between black people born and raised in the United
States and those who are from the continent of Africa; these national
groups cannot be collapsed into each other. Identity confusion can
arise through perceived links with Africa. For instance, the connections with Africa in the United States have sometimes been promoted
by black nationalists who used such images to carve out a separate
black identity. "African American nationalists have taken the lead in
resurrecting and inventing African models for the African diaspora in
the United States. . . . Black nationalists have always argued persua-
sively that African Americans deny their connections to Africa at the
peril of allowing a racist subtext to circulate without serious challenge."[5]

Further, some black nationalists have labeled the black people
who did not jump on their Africa bandwagon as "sick," drawing on
folk healing ideas that determined wellness by relationships. The of-
ten-complex ideas that African Americans have held about Africa are
indicative of conflict that is internal to black communities. This con-

flict is historically based. Black descendants of slaves recognize their unwilling immigration to the United States. With that history in mind, what should the relationships between these descendants and their native lands and forced adoptive land be? What does it mean to be healed of such a past?

A focus on determining proper relationships with Africa is not the extent of healing needed; for African Americans there are also relationships with white America that are in need of remedy. Diagnosing a state of sickness at the beginning of the twentieth century, W. E. B. Du Bois described black American experiences as brokenness, a dissociated state that impaired the resultant quality of life. "It is a peculiar sensation, this double consciousness, this sense of always looking at one's self through the eyes of others, of measuring one's soul by the tape of a world that looks on in amused contempt and pity."[6] Each black person, Du Bois asserted, is torn in two directions: wanting to fully develop talent but caught in hatred from the white American public. Du Bois wrote of the black experience: "This waste of double aims, this seeking to satisfy two unreconciled ideals, has wrought sad havoc with the courage and faith and deeds of ten thousand thousand people,—has sent them often wooing false gods and invoking false means of salvation, and at times has even seemed about to make them ashamed of themselves."[7]

This kind of demoralizing experience demands healing. Du Bois's solution to the dilemma, as he described it nearly one hundred years ago, was one attempt at such a remedy. "He simply wishes to make it possible for a man to be both a Negro and an American, without being cursed and spit upon by his fellows, without having the doors of Opportunity closed roughly in his face. . . . To be a co-worker in the kingdom of culture, to escape both death and isolation, to husband and use his best powers and his latent genius."[8] Such a solution was an oversimplification, however, as will be seen shortly.

The need to heal from dissociations, to become whole in one's identity, is reflected through black-initiated revisions that reflect folk belief in the power of naming. Names are important in black communities, as may be seen in daily life. Family traditions of naming reflect this idea, as for example, the retention of last names and in the use of African names for newborns.

Naming provides connections to family and to ancestors in a world that has pulled black families apart. The retention of women's birth names after marriage, such as Ida Wells Barnett; Frances Ellen Watkins Harper; Mary McCleod Bethune; Bernice Johnson Reagon, has long been a tradition in black communities, a sign of family connection and pride. Sometimes first names are passed from generation to generation. My family tree on my father's side is littered with Andersons and Nancys. Some families will assert that a particular child is an ancestor reborn. The sense of connectedness with ancestors has clear epistemological links with African thought and folk healing beliefs.

Because names are not held lightly in black communities, changing names is serious business. To change the name of a people likewise connotes a serious interior change. A Negro spiritual declares, "I told Jesus it'd be all right if He changed my name," indicating a level of personal commitment. In the nineteenth century, Sojourner Truth chose her own name because she came to understand herself as a person always on a journey in search of the truth. In the twentieth century, Malcolm declared that his surname was "X" as a statement about his sociopolitical relationships in this country.

In like manner, black Americans have worked to come to some community consensus about who "we" are. Some older black people continued to use the name *colored* well into the middle of the twentieth century. The term is still used to retain historic connections by the organization National Association for the Advancement of Colored People. The name "Negro" came to be used and was held with pride by some generations because it was considered respectful in contrast to "nigra" and other derogatory appellations. It is still used by the National Council of Negro Women, reflecting the history of the organization. By the 1960s, "black" was a name that represented self-determination, self-esteem, and defiance, all necessary traits for the healing of African Americans as a people within the United States. The term "Afro American" began to be used in the 1970s, indicating the African origins of black people, an attempt to heal history for those who had been ripped from their homeland. The term "African American" was a further refinement of that same sentiment, connoting the continental origins more strongly (African) rather than as a diminutive (Afro).

In the 1960s, with Black Power consciousness on the rise, these group names were accompanied by sloganeering. "Black is beautiful" was used to counter negative descriptions of black people. Rhythm and blues performer James Brown turned "I'm black and I'm proud" into a song. The Negro National Anthem was revived in the late six-ties and strongly promoted through college Black Studies programs. A raised fist became symbolic of black defiance and self-determination. Each of these names was involved with the efforts to heal the rela-tionships of black communities with America. There was no single conjurer at the forefront of these name changes; it was the conjuring power of identity, which is consistent with traditional folk healings conceptualizations. The group name changes did serve to bring many black Americans to a new awareness that assisted their development.

At the same time, old names have lingered and become weap-ons for personal attack. Anthropologist Annie Barnes has researched black-middle-class experiences of racism and found that derogatory name-calling predictably rankled: "Calling a black person 'colored' is as old and prevalent a slur as calling a black male 'boy.' For decades blacks have not identified their ethnic group as colored. Yet, amaz-ingly, many of the students in my study told me about white people they encountered who have never learned either to pronounce the word *Negro* correctly or to call them by the right title."[9]

Names alone cannot bring healing. Full healing necessitates fully identifying the deeper problems. What is sick in relationships between African Americans and the rest of the country? Can simply insuring civil rights and access to goods and services solve the "illness"?

At the same time, African Americans' experiences and race and the call for healing, the push toward integration that the civil rights movement yielded have resulted in American "one-dimensionality," social critic Adolph Reed Jr. has concluded. Reed contends that cul-tural differences are being homogenized in this climate "There is more than a little irony that the civil rights movement demanded for blacks the same 'eradication of otherness' that had been forced upon immi-grant populations."[10] The processes of assimilating black people have not included finding ways to heal the brokenness of the past.

Folk healing in the twenty-first century offers a thread of resist-ance to what Reed calls "massification," that is, eliminating black par-ticularity by forcing assimilation into Americanized homogeneity. Peo-ple like Ann and Sokara resist this trend by applying creativity to bal-ance and renew life rather than being pushed into the masses. These women and other African Americans selectively draw from the com-mercial culture to add to their ideas of fully living in the world. Such conscious living reflects another form of folk healing by countering the general American climate of one-dimensionality. In so living, they perform another kind of naming ceremony.

Reparations and Reconciliation

The call for reparations, seeking restitution for systematic abuse and oppression, represents another healing action on the part of some black Americans. Some make claims as descendants of enslaved Africans; others consider the entire period of Jim Crow (through 1954) in need of restitution; still others point to black people's inventions or their innovations that have never been recognized or compensated. Exactly who would receive the bill for reparations has been the subject of several proposals. A number of still-operating U.S. companies, such as insurance companies, clearly benefited from enslavement. The U.S. government, others assert, should be held liable and should use tax dollars or higher-education programs as remuneration.

Reparations are not a new idea in the United States. Even before there was a legal end to enslavement, there were discussions about what to do about black people. Suggestions ranged from repatriating the descendants of Africans to settling black people on selected land. Nearly one hundred fifty years past the ending of legal slavery in the United States, no reparations have been made.

The healing aspects of reparations efforts focus on the experiences of alienation and brokenness of Africans in America—barely wanted, usually dropped into a category of "Otherness." But it was not merely psychological pain that was undergone. Civil rights activist Fannie Lou Hamer spoke eloquently before a congressional subcommittee in September 1965, after passage of the Voting Rights Act, of experiences that included physical harm. The committee meeting had been scheduled to address challenges to election results that had excluded the votes of black people in Mississippi.

> I am standing here today suffering with a permanent kidney injury and a blood clot in the artery [in] the left eye from a beating I got inside of the jail in Winona, Mississippi, because I was participating in voter registration and these orders was ordered by a county deputy, a state highway patrol. . . . It is only when we speak what is right that we stand s a chance at night of being blown to bits in our homes. Can

we call this a free country, where I am afraid to go to sleep in my own home in Mississippi?[11]

Hamer's words are dramatic, speaking to the tensions of another time. They are dramatic reminders of the legacy of abuse that black Americans underwent, understanding that photos of Emmett Till's broken body could have been that of any one of them. The sense of possible threat has not ended for black Americans. Whether hearing a of black man's being dragged to death in Jasper, Texas, in the 1990s or a black kindergarten girl's being dragged off in handcuffs in Florida in 2005, the threat of physical harm is a daily event in most black lives. More than forty years after the passage of the National Civil Rights Voting Act, the need for healing remains.

Randall Robinson, a black journalist, commentator, and founder of TransAfrica, begins *The Debt*, written in 2000, with a story of his own pain during a visit to Washington, D.C. Robinson was struck that there are no black faces represented in the memorializing of American heroes and founders, the very absence telling its own story. Reminiscent of W. E. B. Du Bois's sense of being divided, Robinson declares: "I was born in 1941, but my black soul is much older than that. I am this new self and an ancient self. I need both to be whole. Yet there is a war within, and I feel a great wanting of the spirit."[12] Robinson's words resonate with ideas of folk healing, as he aims for wholeness by drawing on an ancestral vision.

Reparations are the focus of the National Coalition of Blacks for Reparations in America (NCOBRA). NCOBRA is based in Washington, D.C., and has been in existence since 1989. Its efforts have been unremitting and their impact is diffused throughout the United States. The current slogan of NCOBRA is "America Must Atone, Reparations Now." Atonement is defined as "Acknowledgement/Apology + Restitution/Reparations." As part of its mission statement in 1995, NCOBRA adopted certain understandings:

Historically the U.S. government has participated in one of the greatest holocausts of human history, the Holocaust of African Enslavement. . . . It has yet to acknowledge this horrific destruction or to take steps to make amends for it. . . . We call on the government of this country to address the morally compelling issue of the Holocaust [by] a) publicly admit[ting] its role . . . b) publicly apologiz[ing] . . .

c) . . . establishing institutions and educational processes which preserve the memory of it . . . d) pay reparations and e) discontinue any
and all practices which continue its effects.[13]

Payment is but a portion of the aims of NCOBRA. The call for ad-
herence to moral standards and to admit and apologize for black oppression reflects the aims of folk healing to balance and renew life, especially through correcting broken relationships. Oppression of black
people did not happen only in the United States. Racism and its effects
are not exclusive to the United States. Profound links are forged across
the African Diaspora.

African Diaspora groups that seek healing from the effects of racism have been able to address these issues in a public and formal
manner. The World Council Against Racism, Racial Discrimination,
Xenophobia, and Related Intolerance in 2001 issued a declaration
against racism and its effects. Although the document took a global
view that included all forms of racism against any people, there was
particular resonance with broad healing concepts.

For those of African descent—the African Diaspora—the long-
term, unaddressed consequences of histories of enslavement and socially embedded racism were detailed by the council: "With a view to
closing those dark chapters in history and as a means of *reconciliation
and healing,* we invite the international community and its members to
honour the memory of the victims of these tragedies."[14] It continued
by declaring that it follows that "as a pressing requirement of justice,"
those who have suffered under the extended effects of racism "should
be assured of having access to justice, including legal assistance where
appropriate, and effective and appropriate protection and remedies,
including the right to seek just and adequate reparation or satisfaction for any damage suffered as a result of such discrimination."[15]
NCOBRA, not surprisingly, concurs with the council's call for reparations and uses the council's declaration to bolster its own arguments.

Reparation movements do not seek recompense simply as a matter of equalizing the distribution of wealth, assets, and goods in the
country. Reparations proposals for black slavery/Jim Crow are primarily aligned with the goals of folk healing. The constant breaking of
African American trust and spirit require healing that money cannot
buy. Money may be a symbol of acceptance and a sign of the offer of
full citizenship. The larger aim is to reach reconciliation, the healing

of broken parts of the country. A parallel action was taken in South Africa when the Truth and Reconciliation Commission there was established. Through the commission, the brutalized confronted their oppressors in formal settings.[16]

Of course, such a commission would not work in the United States context. However, from an African cognitive orientation, healing will happen only when some type of dialogue occurs. Imagine what would happen in the United States if such a commission were established to bring black people who experience oppression into formal sessions with those they feel oppress them (not all of whom are white)? What kind of honesty would be required in this country? If such honesty is healing for black Americans, what would it be for white Americans?

Often white Americans respond to enslavement and Jim Crow from a solipsistic time frame: "*I* did not personally enslave anybody, and therefore I should not be blamed." The result of such a response to others' pain is the continuation of American divisiveness. If white Americans did operate with an African American healing epistemology, their responses to problematical situations would be markedly different. Ecological problems such as global warming or illnesses that primarily afflict white people would be understood to be the results of relationships out of balance, especially stemming from wrongs committed by white ancestors. To heal the present, members of affected communities would be invited to participate in a ceremony designed by religious leaders. At the appointed time, all groups would meet at a symbolic location to recognize the errors of the past and spiritually seek healing. This may seem farfetched within a traditional white epistemological framework, but it is exactly the customary route for black Americans to address past grievances, as seen in the next section.

To the River

African Americans often create healing rituals to bridge the past into the present. And folk healing is the base from which such healing springs. Healing of the past in the present is performed in rituals that utilize nature and link living African Americans with dead and mostly unnamed slaves. One such ritual took place on July 3, 2004.

The Ashé Cultural Arts Center in New Orleans, Louisiana, has

worked with several local organizations to hold a ritual event for the
past years. The other organizations involved cut across religious or
political lines and include the Men of Nehemiah; the Institute of Black
Catholic Studies; the Audubon Institute; the Congo Square Foundation; Liberation Zone Ministries; the Nation of Islam; the People's Institute for Survival and Beyond; and the New Orleans Jazz and Heritage Foundation. Under the Cultural Arts Center's leadership, the
organizations have pooled resources to come together to create an
alternative celebration and ritual around the 4th of July that honors
the sacrifices of African American ancestors. The date of the annual
event is deliberate because many would question the "freedom" black
Americans celebrate today. (One participating organization handed
out copies of a Frederick Douglass speech that challenged the meaning of the 4th of July to the slave.)

Several features of folk healing are part of the occasion: connecting with ancestors (in this case, the enslaved brought through the har-
bor of New Orleans); drawing on nature; awareness of connections
between all the living; and the performance of ritual. The name of the
occasion is MAAFA: International Middle Passage Remembrance and
Renewal Day. "Maafa" is a Kiswahili word that means "great disas-
ter." It is used by some African Americans to describe the Atlantic
slave trade so as to capture its magnitude and impact. Maafa events
around the country also aim to educate the public about the nature of
enslavement and the transatlantic slave trade. These educative reasons
are secondary; the primary purpose of an event is for each participant's benefit. Just as Sokara had helped the man face anger issues
springing from an ancestral memory of enslavement, participants in
an event are invited to face their individual and collective issues
around enslavement. The ceremony does not make the past disappear
but puts it into new perspective.

The New Orleans event is not the only one of its kind. Maafa ceremonies have become routes to memorializing the Middle Passage,
bringing an awareness of how the majority of black Americans' ancestors arrived on these shores. The ceremonies are held in various large
cities throughout the country, including events in San Francisco, Seattle, and Baltimore. One well-known annual event is the Maafa Suite,
produced in September in Brooklyn, New York, at the St. Paul Community Baptist Church.

The New Orleans Ashé Cultural Arts Center was the lead organization sponsoring the Maafa event that I attended. The center produces community-based music, theater, and visual arts events. When I was there in 2004, the center's art exhibit had as its theme, "Healing Genocide," evocative of Ellison's description of the blues. The exhibit addressed violence in the black community with visual arts, closing a month later with another ritual, a traditional New Orleans–style jazz funeral to "bury" violence. Such themes are integral to the work of the center and were reflected in the Maafa Remembrance.

The Remembrance began at 6:00 A.M. in Congo Square (the site of a major slave market). An altar had been erected, using traditional African symbols. Participants were invited to wear white because white is used in traditional African religions' ceremonies to signify protection for the wearer. Speeches from different perspectives were made. Members of the Nation of Islam, the Ausar Auset Society, and Voudoo offered prayers. A Native American minister connected the genocide of black Americans with that of First Nation peoples.

Drummers and dancers then led the way through a Door of No Return that had been erected in the square (see photo at beginning of chapter). The door evoked the name given to compounds at ports on the African continent that held captives for deportation to various colonies. At those ports, the exit from the holding chamber from which captured Africans were herded into ships has been called the Door of No Return.

On that hot morning, all of us participants followed the drummers in procession through the streets to a Mississippi River park. There, after prayer by members of the Institute of Black Catholic Studies, poetry, and music, we went to the river bank and threw white flowers on the water in memory of the African ancestors who had been brought there as slaves. Such a ritual is emblematic of attempts to heal historic social ills through African American folk healing practices.

In African American folk healing, the cosmological view connects the physical, emotional, and spiritual; ancestors with descendants; nature with humans; humans with one another and the Divine. Rupturing any of these relationships results in sickness, which can be physical but may take mental, emotional, or spiritual form. Healing is effected in repaired and restored relationships, enabling a better future. In the Maafa ceremonies, the past is remembered to heal the present.

The social problems in black communities, and in the United States generally, are ills traced to ruptures in the past.

There are other instances in black communities in addition to Maafa remembrances where the past/present healing can be viewed. One is the use of the Black or Negro National Anthem. This hymn is often used in black community gatherings, including black American churches. In the early twentieth century, James Weldon Johnson penned the words; his brother John Rosamond Johnson composed the music. Both brothers had been well educated. James W. had gone to Atlanta University, becoming the first black person to pass the bar in Florida. John R. also had matriculated at Atlanta University, later studying at the New England Conservatory of Music. The anthem's words speak of past pains: "Stony the road we trod, bitter the chastening rod, Felt in the days when hope unborn had died." That pain gives way to "victory" through faith in God coupled with personal and communal steadfastness. The song, given new vigor during the development of black studies programs in the 1960s, conveys a sense of being connected with the ancestors in this moment, pointing again to the future.

The healing power of the Maafa ceremonies stemmed as well from the use of multiple religious traditions, utilizing an array of spiritual resources in the service of black survival. These resources address personal and communal pain, loss, and confusion, and have functioned historically into the present. By creating rituals to address the past and by using a multireligious approach, several insights are made clear. The first is that we African Americans tend to be very pragmatic in our religious lives, using whatever is needed to convey a holistic view of creation. Parts of this holistic view may fall outside most Christian religions' framework, such as intimate connections between humans and nature. But ways to express this view are still found. Second, rituals such as the Maafa ceremonies embrace a culturally grounded view that easily cuts across denominational lines, as the range of participants indicated. This points to an active dimension of African American spirituality that aids the sense of connection among black people. Hence, through these expressions, folk healing adds a level of creativity to the search for the healing of social ills by addressing the participants' needs for commemoration of the past while moving forward to a more positive future.

peans have discovered it over and over: the more they put their foot down, the more we [African Americans] sang."

African American folk healing concepts are influential in understanding Mahdi's system, as Mahdi's life story demonstrates. He drew from folk healing concepts about how the universe is balanced, with human, nature, and the Divine (the spiritual) in necessary and mutual connection with one another. To be out of balance is to be ill. His idea of cooperation highlights the concept of relationality that is so central to African American folk healing. This relationality includes connecting the spiritual to the physical so that their interdependence can be seen in human relationships. Mahdi focuses on folk healing concepts that strive for a balanced universe because the nature of illness stems from ruptures in relationships between humans, or nature, or the spiritual. In this view, it follows that healing is possible by correcting those ruptures. What Mahdi deems to be at stake in a refusal to heal is the genuine achievement of our full power as humans.

This chapter considered questions of identity, reparations, and organized ways in which African American folklore is infused into black life and culture today. The practices of folk healing match the times —no longer primarily agrarian, African Americans creatively apply healing and conjuring to contemporary situations. Maafa ceremonies and healing organizations would not have made sense in the 1970s but they do today. Just as this chapter's opening showed, the old folk practices to heal and protect have not disappeared. Both old and new forms operate in African American communities.

The infusion of folk healing in black communities underscores two characteristics of folk traditions that serve as grounding for this chapter. The first returns to the historical point that African American cultural traditions do not easily fit into white American frames. The second is that many of the aspects of African American folk healing also pertain to religious beliefs. Spirituality is an integral and underlying feature of folk traditions. Humans are not seen as isolated but always in connection with the cosmos, bringing power to the individual and to the community. These ideas are explored in chapter 6.

A candle shop in Detroit connected to a church and run by the pastor offers blessed money plants, elephants, and thinking caps. (Photo taken by author.)

6

Religion, Spirituality, and African American Folk Healing

Several college-age students explained how to keep the night hag away. Sometimes, during a nightmare, you know at some level what is happening and try to wake. But you can't, you feel trapped, and the terror grows. The night hag is making this happen, trying to keep you in the nightmare. Keep the night hag away by placing a broom under the bed. Then she has to stop and count the broom straws and is unable to get into your nightmare. One of the students told me later: "She hasn't gotten me in a long time."

—Conversation in Columbia, South Carolina, 2005

African American religion, sometimes categorized under the rubric "the black church," is intimately tied to the black spirituality. They are not the same but are connected in many ways, and the connections have implications for folk healing. Ethicist Barbara Holmes, discussing what she terms a black contemplative tradition, characterizes the black church in ways that have relevance in relation to folk healing.

The black church has an actual and meta-actual form. It inhabits the imagination of its people in ways that far exceed its reach. Although it is no longer a truly invisible institution, it will always be invisible to some extent because it embodies a spiritual idea. . . . The black church is in a sense "virtual" space created by the worship practices of the congregation.[1]

Holmes identifies some of the changes in the black church over the years, such as streamlining services, and finds the public too often considers black worship restricted to a building and a weekly event.

The black church and black religious practices are not confined to

buildings. Although there are changes in structured worship and organization styles that have occurred over history, it is worthwhile to
remember that black people have cultural patterns beyond the cathar-
tic experiences of singing and shouting that inform religious life.
Holmes identifies a key element of the larger religious practice in ties
to African patterns: "African indigenous religions do not divide the
world into rigid categories; instead religion is deemed to be holistic
and grounded in everyday life."[2] Even as African patterns provide orientation to black American religiosity, the spirituality that grounds African American folk healing has roots in the life of the United States as
well.

Religions are in constant dialogue with the cultures in which their
members live. Because cultures are permeable, cross-cultural experiences inform religions. A brief example will clarify. My daughter and I
lived during her childhood in Detroit, which has strong Polish communities throughout the city. So my daughter came to expect Packzis
on Fat Tuesday and a butter lamb at our family's Easter dinner table.
These cultural religious symbols would have been very different had
she grown up in, say, Louisiana. Regardless of our family's faith profession, culture played a role. The intricate dance between religion and
culture can result in both changing, manifesting hybridity in action.
Spirituality that exists in cultures can come to be expressed in religions, resulting in hybrid forms of religions, cultures, or spiritualities.
These kinds of exchanges have consistently happened throughout the
development of African American folk healing. Because folk healing
rests on a holistic spirituality—connecting physical and spiritual life
with other humans, living and dead, with nature, and with divinity—
spiritual concepts influence the shape and location of healing.

Folk healing's holistic spirituality is developed in creative ways. It
draws on past knowledges and is incipient in its ability to change or
hybridize. Ultimately, folk beliefs contain what Laura Jarmon terms
the *ethos* of black life. She defines "ethos" as "as set of values inherited, binding, and authoritative. . . . Because beliefs, values and ethos
are the bedrock of personal and group identity, they are the foundation of human feeling."[3] This is clearly seen in the development of
black religion.[4]

As enslaved Africans came to adopt new religions—predomi-
nantly Christian—their African-derived spiritualities were retained.

The historical developments of New World African-based religions make this point clear because they easily grew up beside Christianity. Vodou and Candomblé nurtured African spiritualities through Catholic Christianity as devotion to saints masked the worship of divinities known as *loa* and *orixas*. Hoodoo and conjure masked some aspects of African-derived spiritualities that were dismissed as mere superstition by whites. Other aspects of folk healing were blended into and expressed in the contexts of black Christian churches.

Zora Neale Hurston makes this point explicit in her discussion of black worship. Black spirituality retains the idea of visions, particularly as a call to conversion or to preach.[5] Shouting, "an emotional explosion, responsive to rhythm," Hurston identifies as a retention of African "possession by the gods."[6] She read these as signs that

> [t]he Negro has not been christianized as extensively as is generally believed. The great masses are still standing before their pagan altars and calling old gods by a new name. As evidence of this, note the drum-like rhythm of all Negro spirituals. All Negro-made church music is dance possible. The mode and mood of the concert artists who do Negro spirituals is absolutely foreign to the Negro churches.[7]

Many independent black churches were the primary organizations operated by African Americans prior to the end of legal enslavement. Despite white scrutiny, black churches served as meeting places and centers for social life under the constricted conditions of enslavement and legal segregation. Religious denominations of black Christians transformed some aspects of theology while infusing worship with their own cultural styles. Theologian Gayraud Wilmore notes: "It is not possible to speak of Christianity in the United States without recognizing *African American Christianity* as a unique gift of black folk, a Christianity that is the same and yet different from the North American modality of the religion and civilization that claims to revere and model the life, death, and resurrection of Jesus Christ."[8]

Healing practices were not automatically folded into black church worship. Charismatic practices, such as "getting the Holy Ghost," or as Hurston referred to it, spirit possession, were part of some churches. But black churches had their own identity issues. How much black culture should be included in formal worship? Evelyn Brooks Higgin-botham describes this period in black history:

> As time and schooling distanced African Americans further and fur-ther from their slave past, many became self-conscious, conflicted, even critical of the culture of their forebears. From gentle persuasion to ridicule and punishment, white and black missionary teachers sought the demise of the older forms of singing and worship.[9]

Popular culture was most often locked out of the sanctuary, even as African-oriented spirituality continued to inform worship. After the Black Power and civil rights movements of the 1960s, however, re-trieval of black culture was a central focus for many African Ameri-cans. Additionally, the Black Power movement challenged the role of black churches. Out of the dialogue between leaders of the movement and black theologians, black liberation theology was born. One of the primary voices in this development was black theologian James Cone, who wrote,

> Black theology, then, was not created in a vacuum and neither was it simply the intellectual enterprise of black professional theologians. Like our sermons and songs, black theology was born in the context of the black community as black people were attempting to make sense out of their struggle for freedom. In one sense, black theology is as old as when the first African refused to accept slavery as consis-tent with religion.[10]

The 1960s, then, brought different levels of the culture / religion dia-logue. But suspicion of religion, Christianity specifically, as a block to black social progress, continues for some African Americans.

Healing practices had their own path of acceptance that crossed into churches as well as popular culture. Healing was performed often in the Bible. The need to heal the "sin-sick soul" could be expressed in musical forms in church. It was well known that Jesus healed persons, with the promise to heal nations. Thus, in spite of early attempts to divorce the black church from other aspects of black culture, healing was frequently considered appropriate and proper in black church communities. As black congregants wrestled with their American

identities, the healer could be welcomed as easily as the preacher—
and the pastors could conjure healing for their church communities.

Conjure and (Faith) Healing

Conjure requires faith, not in a particular divine being but in the efficacy of the healing work that is being done. The work of healing is not
related only to illness in this context but includes protection from possible harm. The night hag preventive is an example of folk healing as
protection. This kind of protection is available to all who know the
correct formula. Belief in conjure with its use of natural products requires faith in the interconnectedness of the universe. The lodestone
will draw the desired thing or person to the believer; the asafetida bag
worn around the neck will repel disease. Many African Americans believe that they have witnessed the efficacy of such products. Even
among African Americans who do not practice or believe in conjure,
reactions range from fear to outright rejection. But the knowledge of
the practices is prevalent throughout many black communities.

Can conjure or hoodoo legitimately be classed with religion? The
answer to this question is not clear-cut. Yvonne Chireau states:

> Historically, many black Americans have not separated magical be-
> liefs from religion, seeing that the two exist as necessary counter-
> parts. Beliefs in Conjure have not precluded and acceptance of Chris-
> tianity as a complementary system of practice. Conjure coexists with
> Christianity because it is an alternative strategy for interacting with
> the spiritual realm.[11]

A new belief system has been created that is rooted in black American
experiences and reflective of black cultures while retaining African-
derived concepts.

Hoodoo's relationship with faith healing, African Americans' will-
ingness to experiment with religious constructions, and hybrid faith
forms that have developed over the years, are tied to another aspect of
the folk healing. In light of the Black Power movement, organized religion became a stumbling block for some African Americans. The
movement pointed to the historic racism of Christian churches, which

constructed theologies that dehumanized black people. It challenged black people's inability to fully express their distinctive cultural voice in these contexts. The cultural climate of black communities developed so that healing black religion meant searching for African religious traditions.

Healing Religions: Traditional African Religions

Black people across the Diaspora frequently seek healing from the internal divisions they experience when their lived experiences and practices do not match the majority culture. Their need to rediscover a sense of self and community identity becomes particularly profound in the search for religious meaning.

For people of African descent, the draw of traditional religions is reflected in the words of Malidoma Somé, a West African, as he was initiated into Dagara in a region of Burkina Faso:

> The emptiness that had filled me when I had joined the group over thirty days ago, and the suffering I had undergone to achieve true arrival, now seemed justified. I was full. I felt content, oriented, and unconcerned. I was home. . . . As long as we are not ourselves, we will try to be what other people are. . . . During the Dagara initiation process, I grew into myself.[12]

Somé has several scholarly degrees, but these were not enough to fulfill him. The sense of wholeness derived from taking part in African traditional religions related in the previous statement resonates with the experiences of many African Americans who want to find a religious home. Part of this desire relates to a need for healing. Therefore, some African Americans have found their way into forms of traditional African religions.

Iyanla Vanzant is a noted self-help author and speaker who has been initiated into an African American Yoruba-based tradition. Luisah Teish, also initiated into a Yoruba religion, is an author and speaker who explains and explores African spirituality.[13] Teish, like many African Americans who are searching for religious meaning, draws from multiple African traditions to construct and define a spiritual tradition.

For some, then, African religions reconcile seemingly disparate parts of the self—culturally, religiously, and socially. Part of the attraction is what theologian Joseph Murphy describes as "the reciprocity between community and spirit."[14] For some, there is a sense of belonging and coming home. In a way, the participant constructs his or her core identity.

I interviewed one African American woman who has reflected deeply on the meanings of her participation in both Catholicism and African-derived traditions. Renee is an African American artist in her mid-thirties whom I interviewed in a Detroit suburb in February 2005. In her quiet voice, she explained how she began to develop her spirituality. Her mother "was into astrology, loved myths and fairy tales, gypsy and witch stuff." Although Renee had been raised as Catholic, appreciating prayer to the saints and Mary, she was disillusioned by church practices. "Roman Catholicism stopped making sense," she said. Western Christianity has gotten away from the experiential, "It no longer moves you. This is why people are drawn to the evangelical or to Wicca."

Renee began to practice Wicca but also started reading about African religions. "The Craft moved me emotionally, but not enough. . . . The Craft is beautiful in its own right." There are also those who follow the way of Druids, harking back to Celtic religious roots. Others attempt to reconstruct Kemetic rites from Egypt. "But they're still learning how to bring a deity in, move energy—but we've never lost it [in Santería]."

In 1998, Renee was initiated into Santería. "Thank God for the Cubans who saved it for us." For her, Santería is "the foundation; giving everything else a place to rest on. I now have high expectations. It's made the bar [for understanding other religions] really high." She continues her involvement in Santería and states that it is "active living" for her. But Renee also came to practice and be involved in hoodoo because "This is mine for real."

Hoodoo was available to her through study of the works of authors such as Robert Farris Thompson and Luisah Teish. Moreover, as an artist, she studied how the BaKongo people understand the appearances of the deity. She relates that she learned that the "names of things are more important than the thing." She studied African enslavement and the cultures and religions from the people's places of origin. She learned about where ideas of spirits and "haints" derive in black folk knowledge.

Renee asserts that hoodoo is not dead but is "undergoing a transformation." People can find information online and are trying to mix different forms. She has no nostalgic feelings for the hoodoo of the past. "It's not gone, it's gone in its old form. We don't live in those days. We can't [walk up to someone and] blow powder in their face. . . . After the great migration, it had to change. The heart of it has to change. . . . Hoodoo is very flexible." Renee notes that today, urban hoodoo is the type that exists in city centers. However, she cautions that a "commercialization of hoodoo . . . is coming. [We see that] the Native American, goddess, and Celtic fads have all played out," so new spiritual products will be sought by the public.

Renee, like many others, has been willing to examine her faith and spirituality, looking for what brings meaning and coherence to her life. Her story reflects the searching patterns of many African Americans, some of whom find their answers in organized religions. But many black people express their spiritual truths in other ways. For Renee, the best way of expressing herself was not in the Catholic Church, where she felt something missing. She wanted the experiential dimension but was unfulfilled in Wicca. She has found a sense of peace in the spiritual expressions—Santería and hoodoo—that she identifies as culturally relevant and connected with her past.

There is no uniformity or unanimity among practitioners of traditional African religions or hoodoo. One area that creates dissention among practitioners of traditional African religions in the United States is animal sacrifice, which is required for some rituals. Sokara (cited in chapter 4) delineated reasons for this difference during her interview:

> I had tried that other route, [the traditional African ancestral reverence and so forth]. I didn't find it an evolved process in the way a lot of African Americans are doing it. And I had many arguments or debates with people who were teachers in that tradition. I'm a vegetarian and I'm not comfortable with animal sacrifice. It may have been necessary five thousand years ago. It's not now. We're evolving. . . . Just as we human beings are coming into cosmic consciousness, animals are coming into self-consciousness. All of creation is evolving. I didn't find it acceptable that an animal's life was being sacrificed for spiritual purposes.

I have heard variations of Sokara's statement from other African American practitioners of African religions. They reflect the tensions between African practitioners of their religions and American adaptations of these religions. Renee, when I interviewed her, contended that African religions are thriving among black people in the United States and dying off on the African continent. But to fit into an American framework, adaptations are taking place.

The processes of the adaptation of African to Americanized versions are manifested in the dynamics of the Òyótúnjí African Village, which has been in Sheldon, South Carolina since 1970. Central to the life of the Village is the Yoruba religion which all community members practice. A sign outside the compound proclaims: "Welcome to Òyótúnjí. You are now leaving the United States of America and about to enter the Yoruba Kingdom of Òyótúnjí African Village." The community has been the focus of many academic studies.

I visited the village for a day in 2004. The tour guide was a young man, still in high school, and filling in as guide for the day. He had lived in the community all his life, had been educated there, and was fully initiated as a member of the religion. Although the number of families residing there is small (thirteen at the time of my visit), a total view of life is adopted. The members adopt a philosophy that is deliberately in contrast to the majority of the country, hence the message on the sign.

The guide explained that the founders and several other members of the community often travel to the African continent, where they learn handicrafts, among which are clay work and sculpture, from African artisans. The residents produce many of their own necessities. One key reason is for the community to be self-sufficient; another is a commitment to living in an African style. Several community buildings are places of worship for various orishas, reflecting a characteristic of African derived religions. "At the center of Afro-Caribbean religions is a belief in a unique Supreme Being—creator of the universe. This belief is complemented by belief in a pantheon of deities (orishas, *loas*, and the like) who are emanations of the Creator and who serve as intermediaries between mankind [*sic*] and the supreme god."[15] As in other buildings in the Village, the residents had built the shrines; some were quite elaborate and included large sculptural representations of the particular deity.

The tour guide commented that very few trips are made to outside doctors; the community uses herbal remedies. The guide himself was not familiar with any; his mother knew "all that."

Anthropologist Kamari Maxine Clarke has written an in-depth study of the village. She discusses the village as "a node in a network of religious revivalists . . . constituted by both cultural and political forms of nationalisms though which to produce new forms of membership."[16] Clarke understands these new networks as "deterritorialized" creators of linkages. The linkages become "transnational communities . . . forged within histories of displacement and [show] how people, in an attempt to forge alliances, produce the term for membership within institutions of power."[17] Clarke's analysis offers a helpful structure for consideration of the parallel and related thinking in the retentions and revivals of African American folk healing.

A distinctive consciousness about the body is reflected in the adoption of African religious practices. For instance, upon the death of a person who has been initiated into one of the traditional African religions, ceremonies for care of the body and recognition of the spirit are used. Certain options, such as cremation, are not permitted. The one who has died becomes one of the ancestors who are then regularly "fed" and given recognition by other members of the community. That ancestral spirit is considered to be present for, and working with members of the immediate family. The community within a traditional African religion is called a house. One's house is a community that cares for one another, closely resembling family membership. Such communal and familial practices related to the body are clearly seen in places where African practices have consistently been present since enslavement, such as Brazilian Candomblé houses. But perhaps part of the attraction of these traditional religions for some African Americans is a sensed absence of community in American society. The coming "home" mentioned by Somé is a powerful draw for people who have experienced being unwelcomed where they live.

For the Òyótúnjí members, the healing effect of religion through adoption of African practices is related to separating the community from mainstream U.S. life. The village is as self-sufficient as possible, eschewing connection to the state of South Carolina's infrastructure: water is from its own wells on the property; lighting is not from sources supplied by the power company; cooking is in fire pits. Members of the village have wage labor commitments, but their income is generally used for the upkeep of all members.

There are questions within the larger African American community regarding whether this kind of divorce from the United States is really workable. The guide could not furnish an estimate of the number of people who have resided at the village since the seventies, though the number is low. An acquaintance who has been initiated into another form of African religion, Santería, is derisive of the village: "Who wants to live in the nineteenth century?" Nevertheless the village communicates something about religious possibilities to other African Americans. The tour guide informed us that many who have been initiated choose not to live in the village, embracing the Yoruban religion but not the lifestyle of the village.

Healing Religion: Creating Alternatives

The adoption of some form of traditional African religions is only one exploration for purposes of healing their religious lives by black Americans. Other creative approaches involve construction of a separate religious denomination, such as the Nation of Islam.

Womanist theologian Delores S. Williams has called for African Americans to analyze the ways religion does or does not work in life:

> An examined faith is a critical way of seeing that shows those things in a belief system that are life-threatening and life-taking. An examined faith inspires people to discard beliefs, images, and symbols that have the potential to support scapegoating and destruction. . . . An examined faith discards any religion and any God who commands Black people to sit idly contemplating love of their oppressors while they (Black people) are threatened and destroyed by those who hate them.[18]

Williams's words express the need that many African Americans have felt: religion itself needs healing. To achieve this aim, some people operate from within their mainstream church communities, bringing in African influences. For instance, it is not unusual to find Presbyterian churches that have African drums throughout the service or a Catholic priest vested in African Kente cloth. Other historically black Christian churches have long had connections to black cultural concepts, such as the African Methodist Episcopal (A.M.E.) church. For others, internal reform of existing Christian denominations has not been sufficient to address the past wherein black people were theologically deemed inferior and the natural-born servants of white people. Rituals, such as the Maafa ceremonies, are sometimes enacted outside organized religions' boundaries. But such practices still may not be sufficient to satisfy the spiritual needs of some black Americans who see a Western spirituality that sharply separates body and spirit, person and community, or human and divine as a form of illness.

The creativity with which African Americans have approached religion works to end such illness. Black people often develop religions as responses to social ills, the establishment of the A.M.E. Church is one of the earliest examples.

> The historic decision that Richard Allen and Absolom Jones made in 1787 to transcend the divisiveness of white denominationalism by organizing a nonsectarian society that could solidify the black community for morality, social welfare, and benevolence led directly to the founding of the AME Church and the Episcopal Church of St. Thomas. . . . Allen at least was ultimately successful in wresting control from whites and establishing one of the first national institutions concerned about the liberation and uplift of all Afro-Americans.[19]

The A.M.E. Church may have been the first, but it was not the last. Black religious creativity has exemplified hybridity in the development of other types of churches. In the early 1920s, for example, the Eternal Life Christian Spiritualist Church began in New Orleans under the direction of Mother Leafy Anderson. Although it was somewhat similar to Spiritualist churches that began in England in the 1800s, it was distinctive because it blended Voudou and Native American religious practices to form a distinctly African American version. These churches, still in existence, also practice healing. The black Spiritualist churches exemplify hybridity in their development, but the Nation of Islam is an example of a religion that focuses directly on workings to heal some aspect of black life.

The Nation of Islam (N.O.I.) originated in Detroit in 1930, when Minister Wallace D. Fard, a traveling merchant, began to preach a new style of religion to the people he served. Fard, who asserted that he had been to Mecca, taught that Islam was the original religion of black people, not Christianity. When Fard disappeared in 1934, the mantle of leadership passed to Elijah Muhammad, who was more militant and successful in drawing converts. Mosques were opened in cities with significant black populations.[20]

The membership of the N.O.I. has traditionally been significantly young, male, lower class, American, and formerly Christian. Group solidarity and race consciousness are N.O.I.'s focus. In his classic text on black Muslims, C. Eric Lincoln cites the aims of group membership as stated by one of the Muslim ministers: "To get the white man's foot off my neck, his hand out of my pocket and his carcass off my back. To sleep in my own bed without fear, and to look straight into his cold blue eyes and call him a liar every time he parts his lips."[21]

Religion is used by N.O.I. to heal identity by situating black people as *not* white and, therefore, clearly defined as a group. "The stress upon—and the outward manifestation of—fraternal responsibility is a strong attraction for many Blacks whose social and civil insecurity is often extreme."[22] The sense of security with answers for every question, such as how family should be structured or how men should act, is an attractive feature for some African Americans who do not find such clarity in other denominations. The N.O.I. can be particularly healing for some sectors of black society, such as black men imprisoned for crimes. Few if any correctional programs have significant rehabilitation programs. Many African American men who are imprisoned end up caught in the revolving doors that return them to prison. And most Christian churches, if they have a prison ministry, do not have the kind of substantive program that is needed. When a convict becomes a member of N.O.I., he is folded into a support group. When he leaves the prison, he is housed and given employment through a host group. He is, as one substance abuse counselor stated, not rehabilitated but oriented into society, as he had not been so oriented previously. Education for life is provided, along with a daily structure and expectations.

Religion itself becomes a form of healing, using components from the black community's imagination in order to address social and political issues. The leadership and creativity of Mother Leafy Anderson, Minister Wallace D. Fard, and many others successfully tap into black religious symbolism and use it in the organizations they build. But folk practices that include curing can most clearly be seen in the processes of faith healing.

Faith and Healing

African American faith healing practices are nurtured in Christian churches that have charismatic practices. Principles of folk healing are incorporated through processes of hybridization, whereby African Americans import and mix practices and beliefs to create something new that is their own. Some question whether such blended practices diminish the legitimacy of the faith professed or are dangerous. I interviewed Linda in 2003, and her story of faith healing is illustrative. Linda had been diagnosed with severe hypertension that no medicine tried had been able to control. She was on a strict regimen that included some experimental medications and weekly visits to her doctor's office.

Linda's adult daughter, "being very religious, told me that her church was having a faith healer that evening. And I had never heard of a faith healer." With her daughter, Linda reluctantly attended the healing service entitled "Lifting up Jesus" at a packed church. When the sick were invited to the sanctuary, her daughter encouraged Linda to go up for healing. After several nudges during the service, Linda began to walk forward:

> And I was so nervous, I remember just shaking in my shoes because I'm thinking to myself . . . I am too sophisticated to be falling on this hard wood floor. . . . I went up to the altar and he [the minister] asked me what did I want him to pray for me about? So I told him my blood pressure and stuff . . . and the medication was not workings. So he said okay, and he raised his hands on my forehead and . . . took some blessed oil on his hands and he put them on my forehead and that was it. All in all I was up there for maybe then or fifteen seconds. . . . I was feeling this sensation in my stomach . . . and it's circling and circling until it covers my whole body. And it was like a hot-cold type of feeling.

After the service, Linda went for her regular doctor's appointment. The doctor said, "Oh, your blood pressure is down, I knew we were going to find something" that worked on the condition. But as Linda's regular visits continued, the doctor could not understand what was going on. "And she [the doctor] looked at me as though . . . I was doing something illegal. . . . She said, 'Your blood pressure, it's normal, it's perfect! What are you doing?'" Linda told her about the faith healing, which did not impress the doctor, who instructed Linda to continue to take her medicine.

That particular week, Linda was preparing to take her medication when she heard a voice: "'Step out on faith.' I heard it. . . . So I put the pills back in the bottle and put them in the medicine cabinet. And the voice said, 'Step out on faith, get rid of the pills.' So I . . . emptied them all in the toilet. . . . I joined the church after that." Linda's blood pressure has been normal since the healing.

Linda's story directly challenges the efficacy of institutional medicine. It upsets some people, who wonder why a reasonable woman with a chronic medical condition would listen to a voice as a way to direct her health care. Was her behavior dangerous and foolish? Was she just lucky that some of the experimental medicine began to work? Her story is upsetting on another level because she was not a member of a church and had never heard of faith healing. She was not a woman of faith, it would seem, yet she experienced healing. What is the relationship between personal faith and healing? The minister did not ask her belief system but inquired after the medical condition she wanted to have healed. Was he functioning more as a conjurer than a minister? Linda's story does not lend itself to easy interpretation but is part of existing African-derived concepts that connect body, soul, the Divine, and nature. The play between religious faith and folk healing can be seen in other black churches as well.

Some black churches directly incorporate healing into their faith practices. The African American Spiritualist churches mentioned above offer key examples of this incorporation, adopting practices and beliefs from "Roman Catholicism, Pentecostalism, nineteenth-century Spiritualism, New Thought, and African religious concepts that were incorporated into what is known as Voodoo or hoodoo in the United States."[23] Anthropologist Claude Jacobs notes that the churches distinguish between illnesses that are natural (physical, psychological, or social) and unnatural ("sorcery, works of the devil or 'seducing' spirits"). Jacobs states that many illnesses are viewed as the result of the mind or thinking self:

This view of the "self" as a cause of problems has influenced Spiritual ministers' ideas concerning the paraphernalia they use (candles, incense, and oils) and the rituals they perform or prescribe (spiritual baths, novenas, and anointings). According to the ministers, such material objects or ceremonies have no intrinsic power but only help to establish belief or faith in the mind.[24]

Jacobs mentions that the ministers around New Orleans are particularly aware of the similarities of their healing practices with conjure and voudou and "are sometimes sensitive about the subject. Nevertheless, there have been and still are Spiritual ministers who claim to use frogs, beef tongues, and chickens in their rituals in ways that parallel descriptions of Voodoo/hoodoo."[25] Such healing practices are sometimes adopted in churches without recognition of the source of those customs.

Betty Price is the wife of the popular and controversial West Coast preacher Frederick Price. Mrs. Price was diagnosed with inoperable malignant cancer in 1990. The cancer was treatable, but Mrs. Price chose differently. "I told [Fred] I did not want to take the chemotherapy or radiation treatments; I was going to believe God for my healing. I told Fred that I did not believe God wanted me to take chemotherapy because it kills your good cells and destroys your body."[26] She acknowledged that in the same time frame, she had been fearful of the treatments. The cancer progressed until the tumor was protruding from her side. She finally agreed to the treatments and offered a new understanding to the followers of the Prices: "God had made a way of escape but it was up to me to trust Him through it. . . . We [she and Fred] never said you do not take medication when you are operating on faith. . . . Your faith is to be based on believing you have received what you asked God for."[27] Mrs. Price now supports the use of doctors, believing that God works through doctors. She also advocates a healthy diet.

Mrs. Price's story reflects two types of faith healing practice. The first is parallel to that of many charismatic churches, black and white. It is passive, depending on God to "take care of" everything. Mrs. Price's first conceptualization of God's work bordered on the magical because minimal human intervention was anticipated and belief was the primary tool for healing, expressed in Bible verses. There was such a clear separation between the Divine and the human that human effort was wasted. This approach is in stark contrast to principles of folk healing because African American folk healing is not passive; rather, its practices use anything at hand that is effective. Mrs. Price's second type of healing practice is more closely allied with African American folk healing. She came to blend medical treatment with daily practices, such as attention to nutrition. She understood doctors as channels for the actions of the Divine. Her ideas are now more holistic, viewing life as more interconnected and interrelated.

Faith Healers

With these differences in the combinations of faith and healing in mind, I interviewed three faith healers, each of whom is grounded in Christianity. If there is a common thread among these women's practices, it is their commitment to their Christian faith. The first two healers are sisters who live in Chicago.

In April 2004, I interviewed Evangelist Earma and Evangelist Cleopatra, both in their sixties. Originally from Mississippi, they had moved with their families to the North. Evangelist Cleopatra gave an indication of the discipline instilled in them as children: "My mama taught us to live a clean life." She has been in relationship with God since she was saved at age sixteen. She clearly remembers this because "when God give you anything, you remember."

The women understand themselves as healers and prayer "warriors." Evangelist Cleopatra, the more loquacious of the two, explained that "the prayer warrior get things from God that the others don't get. . . . A prayer warrior is alert." Both spoke of ways that their relationship with God creates other possibilities in their lives. For instance, Evangelist Earma reported that the Lord might give her someone's phone number to call, which she will do to pray with him or her. Evangelist Cleopatra asserted, "I can't change, I'm in the Word of God," indicating that the relationship between person and the Word is intimate. These spiritual abilities are only possible through God's gift, and, as Evangelist Cleopatra stated, "You don't get this [gift of God] by looking pretty [but by] living a consecrated life to God."

Evangelist Cleopatra spoke about her visions, understanding these as gifts from and communication with God. In 1950, while at prayer, she "saw a vision of a man standing in a field. His hand was in a machine and his left arm was trapped. The Holy Spirit began to speak a prophecy through me of what I had seen in the vision. The very next day my eldest bother lost his left arm in a corn puller machine."[28]

Both women believe that God has given them the gift of healing, which they validate by recounting story after story of their healing people. Evangelist Earma recounted that her sister healed her after she had been diagnosed with first-stage cancer. "My sister came and put some oil on my throat. I went in the bathroom and spit up" a lump. Doctors were not able to find any cancer after that.

Evangelist Cleopatra told how she had healed herself. She had been sick and vomiting throughout the night and began to pray. "Lord, I rebuke that in the name of Jesus." I said it three times. My husband called the doctor. The doctor told him to bring me in [the next day]. I prayed." Others came in pray with her. She said she felt a light enter her body and pass through it. When she went to the doctor, she was given a clean bill of health.

Some of the sisters' stories have humorous twists. Evangelist Cleopatra told of a woman who came to her and said she had a tumor in her head. "I told her she didn't have a tumor, she had stress. She went to the doctor. Guess what he say? . . . she had stress."

Evangelist Cleopatra's distinct memories of receiving God's gift of healing are reflected in her own written account.

> In 1982, the Lord spoke to me and said, "I will put the gift of healing in your hands." He also said that he would instruct me how to pray for [an] individual's specific needs. For example there were times when God would tell me to instruct a soul to drink a cup of water that I prayed for, or to eat a piece of bread from their kitchen after a prayer was offered.

Regarding the work of healing, she asserted, "When God heal you from anything it don't come back. Unless you do what you're not supposed to."

There are certain themes in the women's stories that are both similar to and contrast with African American folk healing traditions and concepts. The most significant theme is their relationships with God. Through God, all their gifts are given; all power comes. Any gifts, like visions, are understood as strictly from God; there is no discussion of personal psychic abilities, such as clairvoyance. Healing is similarly a testimony to God's power alone. When God heals an ill person, as Evangelist Cleopatra declared, the illness will not come back unless the person is doing something that she or he is "not supposed to." This reflects the black mystical tradition that believes in an efficacy-order in the universe with interconnections of all things. God's power channeled through these women is reminiscent of Ann's discussion of energy (chapter 4).

The sisters draw energy for healing from outside themselves. The person of the healer, in the evangelists' view, is the conduit for God's power. Being a conduit is gift itself, a sign of God's choice that bears responsibility. As Ann gives the name *energy* to healing power, so these women name their healing as God's power. To understand healing as from God certainly lends more authority to the healer. Sharply different from folk healing, the responsibility of the healer is based on obedience to God—however that is defined or known. Gifts such as healing are not perceived as neutral but imply the moral uprightness of the healer who is dedicated to fulfilling God's will. For these evangelists, there is no conscious connection to African American folk healing traditions. Such traditions may be cultural vestiges that they blend into their Christian faith. Because of their belief in healing and other charismatic gifts that remain outside the control of any church hierarchy, the Christianity in which the two sisters believe might be unrecognizable to some mainstream Christian denominations. For those denominations, the idea of the women's constant communication with God would be particularly problematic because, for those theological constructions, God's revelation ended with Jesus. To an outsider, what they are doing may appear very similar to folk healing, as the story with Linda's experience of being healed affirms.

I interviewed Shirley, another faith healer, in Ohio in March 2004. In her early forties, she is a minister in the Spiritualist tradition, the tradition founded by Mother Leafy Anderson. Shirley grew up with a sense of being God-touched and was comfortable with her mystical experiences. "I can remember seeing angels when I was younger. I always hear audibly, 'Shirley, don't do that, because you know if you do that, you'll get in trouble.' And I didn't think I was crazy, I just knew that I had somebody watching over me."

Shirley's relationship with her childhood Christian church did not block her exploration of her gifts:

> I was raised Baptist but there was still something missing. I loved the church, it was a big part of my life, but it wasn't getting to what I needed to know, what I needed to feel. What I needed to feel was earth and the energies around it. . . . But I believe in God and I knew God is all there was and all there is. God has always been the first and center of my life. But I knew that there were other things out there. . . . And those avenues have just always been open to me and it just seemed like as I needed the information God put different people into my life.

Shirley sought knowledge, and notes, "Everything I've learned, I've not learned through the black community." She apprenticed as a healer to a white minister whom she describes as an amazing man who was a hands-on healer.

> I got to apprenticeship with him for sixteen years. [The apprenticeship] entailed learning to use the energy around you, the energy through you, and being able to heal through unconditional love. You don't have to like the person, but you have to accept them. And they have to accept their self in order to receive healing. . . . I had to learn to protect myself and not keep what was pulled out of that person. . . . I have seen miracles upon miracles upon miracles with this man. . . . I've seen people who had really bad hearing. It did not come absolutely normal, but it improved. I've seen one lady that was full of cancer and she would have documentation that the doctor said that she had cancer and that he [the doctor] didn't give her but so much time to live. . . . She came in they worked on her for a week, she want back to the doctor. Her doctor said, "Lady, this is what us doctors don't like to discuss. You have not an ounce of cancer in your body."

Shirley related other learning experiences. For instance, she became a skilled herbalist, learning where she could. Her interest in herbal healing, she believes, came from her Native American grandmother, who was a medicine woman. "Her name was Susie, and she could go to the woods and pull out—and I think that's where this need to know about plants and earth, for me, came from, from her. My father would get sick and a lot of times, grandma would come up from Alabama and she'd put poultices on him." Shirley's mother rejected these practices, reflecting the conflict within black communities. "Mama thought they were voodoo. I understand now that they weren't. She [Susie] just went and got some herbs, sometimes have him drink some teas that would draw the sickness out. Mom was really freaking out, she sent grandma home." Shirley went to visit her grandmother only once, when she was twelve. For that single visit, her mother demanded that "[Susie] would not teach us anything, anything whatsoever." Shirley regrets the absence of the knowledge that went to the grave with her grandmother, and has since studied with a local herbalist. She has learned to make tinctures, salves, and poultices; she learned to grow and process a variety of herbs. The course ran several months and was expensive but provided all the seedlings and recipes that helped her begin her home herb garden. At the time of the classes, Shirley interacted with other religious traditions that had also studied herbal lore. "When I went down for that class I met a voodoo princess, there were a couple of Wiccans down there—I am a Spiritualist minister—and so my instructor asked how I felt about all that. But that's their belief, I'm not going to govern their belief. And I'm not going to throw mine down."

Shirley's mother, despite her fears of voodoo, has come to rely on her daughter's skill. Shirley commented, "Now, I laugh because my mother will say, 'Shirley, my knees hurt.' So then I make her a cayenne salve for her knees and back."

In contrast to the evangelists, Shirley has a clear sense of her own power, recognizing her responsibility and actively seeking knowledge. She is Spiritualist but finding what is effective and what works for her life is more important than any commitment to doctrinal purity.

The contemporary uses of folk healing practices signal that black Americans are consciously developing ways to identify knowledge in more formal recognized venues, such as religious ceremonies or healing touch centers. The ideas that shimmer through the narratives of the two evangelists and the healer Shirley are more sharply defined when we recognize the cultural frameworks that underscore their belief systems. Folk healing has been diffuse in black life. This chapter focused on faith and healing; the previous chapter focused on healing black identities. The next chapter turns toward ways that African American folk healing is directly accessible and more visible.

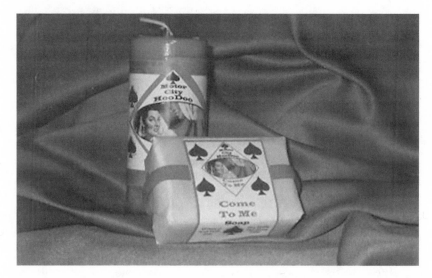

Two of the Motor City Hoodoo products. (Photo taken by author, Ferndale, MI.)

7

Hoodoo, Conjure, and Folk Healing

Recipe for a mojo bag: Into a small cloth bag, add ingredients that are needed to address the situation you wish to alter. So to attract love, add herbs such as cinnamon or orris root; stones such as lodestones or citrine; or flower petals or oils from roses or lavender. Always add ingredients in odd numbers. Close the bag by binding it with thread. Bless the bag (as you wish) and focus your intentions. Keep the bag near you or in a sacred space. "Feed" the bag at least once a week to maintain its power with whiskey, rum, or other selected items until the purpose of the bag is fulfilled. (Mojo bag kits are also available for purchase.)

—From a class on making mojo bags

During my graduate studies, I often brought the new ideas I had learned to my mother's house to discuss with her; her health had started to fail and our time to talk was very important for me. Sometimes the ideas came in book form and I would bring the books and read to her. Once, I brought the *Egyptian Book of the Dead*. I do not remember what I was studying or what I wanted to talk about with her. I do remember that, as the day was ending, we were seated in her living room in the quiet of twilight. I was reading some passage to her, wanting to illustrate some point I was making, when a picture fell off the wall. The walls were solid, the picture was hung securely—but still it fell. My mother's response was immediate: "Stop reading that NOW!"

Folk healing practices continue into the twenty-first century for reasons listed in chapter 3, the end of the first part of this book. If we recall, some of those reasons for their persisting were the marginalization of black Americans because of race and class; the lack of access to institutional medicine; the adaptation of folk healing practices and ingredients; the pragmatic and proven efficacy of the cures; and the holistic approach to the person. An additional reason is the down-to-earth way that culture is transmitted in families and communities. Cultural transmissions are not just ritualized practices; they are mindsets. Notwithstanding my mother's college degree and my own education, it was simply time to stop reading from a sacred book at twilight when a picture falls off the wall because, as my mother admonished, "Don't mess with that stuff!"

A folk healing mindset shapes African American activities. This mindset views the world holistically and considers the connections between all human life, spirits, nature, and the Divine as having power. It is logical, in this mindset, to attempt to heal religions or society. Healing has value in itself because it represents a deeper connection to nature, the Divine, and other humans, and is therefore sought for physical, mental, emotional, and spiritual illnesses. Folk healing practices today look and sound different from the practices described in the Slave Narratives and the WSU Folk Archives. In spite of educational levels, the contemporary practices continue demonstrating a mindset aimed toward healing.

Modernized Versions

We have discussed African American folk healing broadly within larger schemes of black cultural awareness and production. Hoodoo, conjure, rootwork, and juju all provide windows into understanding the broader category of African American folk healing. However, some of the terms need clarification, particularly as they are used today.

Generally the terms "hoodoo" and "conjure" are used interchangeably. As seen in accounts from the Slave Narratives, hoodoo is sometimes dismissed as superstition or may be confused with the religion Voudou. Some African Americans may fear the terms themselves because they are seen as non-Christian. Yet, the practices that would be designated as "hoodoo" are ongoing. Defining hoodoo as non-Christian is an oversimplification that reduces the supernaturalism found within black culture's holistic view to the realm of "evil" magic.

Magic has a wider acceptance in mainstream American culture today and this sets up a context for considering the supernatural that is sharply different from the time when the WSU Folk Archives accounts were collected. On an academic level, magic is also seen differently, particularly as an area for research. For instance, research by Bruno Bettleheim considered the importance of magical thinking for the development of children.

The sharpest difference can be seen in popular culture. The contemporary idea of magic includes everything from dragons to vampires. Exemplifying this difference are the *Harry Potter* series of books and movies, which have been an astounding international commercial success. This success has dismayed some Christian groups that fear the books' and movies' influence over young people. Among religions, other differences can be noted. Pagan and Wiccan groups are formally designated in many places as religions. These religions have been part of the reintroduction of the language of magic into common parlance, including spelling the word as *magick* to indicate its religious meanings and its historical roots. So African Americans, like many others in the nation, might eschew the magic of hoodoo but watch various movies with magical themes.

In the previous chapter, we saw that Renee expected hoodoo's eventual commercialization. She said that this trend is inevitable because other religious fads, like the Druid and Native American religions, have run their course and hit their peak of interest. Whether her expectations of the future materialize remains to be seen; she does have insight that common perceptions of hoodoo reduce it to just another form of magic. Unfortunately, the reduction may occur because magic sells in popular culture.

Limiting hoodoo to magic is misleading. Yvonne Chireau contends that the "magic/religion" dichotomy as well as the "non-Christian" designation given to hoodoo practices does not reflect how African Americans think about religion. Chireau asserts: "Instead of viewing supernaturalism as a marginal subset of African American religion, I have identified supernatural traditions as they appear within and outside black spiritual traditions."[1] Ultimately, she concludes, we should "rethink the categories that we use for looking at religion in the United States today. Rather than considering supernaturalism apart from a social and cultural mainstream, I have placed it at its center."[2]

The continuation of hoodoo among African Americans is part of what has led some black thinkers like Chireau to reconsider hoodoo. Such reconsideration from African American scholars' points of view is neither new nor limited to folk practices. Black scholarship, with particular intensity since the civil rights and Black Power movements of the 1960s, has worked to analyze African American life from black perspectives. This has occurred across academic disciplines, including cultural studies, history, and theology. It means that black life and culture can be reinterpreted from black frameworks based upon the new analyses. For instance, Dwight Hopkins reinterprets the conjurer as an archetypal figure, among other archetypes, for African Americans.[3] His purpose in this analysis is to posit a theological anthropology that is foundational for a holistic black liberation theology. It establishes new boundaries for thinking about the conjurer, expanding beyond superstition or folklore to get at the underpinnings of African American religious thought. The new view of the conjurer can become a window into the use of myth in an African American epistemology.

Such interpretation takes root concepts from African American culture and understands them in the wider field of humanity. This development among African American scholars is very different from what was occurring throughout the Slave Narratives and WSU Folk Archives but is still within an African American intellectual tradition.

In the same way that reinterpretations of African American concepts change our understandings, so too do redefining words. Redefinitions of "conjure" and "hoodoo" have been reintroduced to black and white American audiences. Some of the redefinitions are consistent with historical definitions; some have new shadings or dimensions. A few examples will clarify.

Tayannah Lee McQuillar defines the word "rootwork" in such a way that it encompasses all folk healing practices.

> Rootwork is a form of folk *magick* that uses the elements of nature to create change in ourselves, others, or our environment. It is an African-American form of *shamanism* that makes use of herbs, stones, rocks, and other organic material to heal the body or mind, or to solve a problem. Like all other forms of shamanism, Rootworkers believe that we can use the unseen forces of nature to manipulate the tangible world. Rootwork is also known as "Hoodoo."[4]

McQuillar states that rootwork is not a religion and that "the theology behind the spells has been lost, thus there is no formal initiation to become a rootworker. However, a good practitioner is traditionally referred to as Doctor, Mother, Uncle, or Aunt out of respect for their vast problem-solving knowledge."[5]

In her definition, McQuillar draws from the ideas of other cultures and frames of reference. She uses the term "magick" recalling the Wiccan spelling, and the more formal definition shamanism, which adds wider legitimacy to the idea of rootwork. She recalls naming practices that have historical links that indicate wise and respected members of the community—Uncle, Mother. This hybridized form signals the reader that there is nothing shameful about rootwork. McQuillar is focused on justifying rootwork or folk magick, inviting the reader to participate. She never uses the terms "conjure" or "conjurer," drawing away from those more negatively perceived words. She gives instruction on the use of mojo bags as she lists ingredients for the charm bags and the spells with some limited background information. McQuillar's book is an example of works intending to popularize hoodoo or conjure, which are discussed later in this chapter. As one of those types, her definition is set up to be as nonoffensive to as many people as possible.

Faith Mitchell, a medical anthropologist, refers to hoodoo and conjure with more conventional definitions, as part of a system of black traditional medicine. Mitchell, who has focused her research on Gullah practices in the Sea Islands of South Carolina, distinguishes between natural, occult, and spiritual illnesses. The herbalist who is knowledgeable about roots can treat natural illnesses. Occult illnesses are caused by hoodoo, and the person is considered hexed or crossed. Only a conjurer, who can draw upon natural elements, personal power, and spells to effect a cure, can bring about healing for these illnesses. "A person who is both herbalist and conjurer is frequently called a *root doctor*, and the terms roots and root medicine include hoodoo as well as herbs." Spiritual illnesses, however, require religious healers "capable of channeling the healing powers of God."[6] Mitchell works more closely within African American conceptual frames, unlike McQuillar. But Mitchell is less interested in selling any audience on folk healing and focuses on research about healing work in a specific geographic area. Including spiritual healing from God's powers also resonates in many black Christian communities where conjure and Christianity, as Chireau asserts, operate in interrelated ways.

The use of contemporary terms in its definitions or interpretations aims to make folk healing comprehensible to contemporary minds. Medical anthropologist Eric Bailey places black folk healing within the context of "alternative medicine."[7] Bailey uses the terminology of "alternative" to move black folk healing out of the sensational and into mainstream thought. Unlike McQuillar's work, directed toward a popular audience, Bailey's work aims to educate medical profession-als and students. There is some benefit in getting people to think about black folk healing without fear. There is a decided benefit for Bailey's work because the use of acceptable and familiar terminology may help those working in institutionalized medicine to understand something about folk healing; this may in turn aid in the growth of cultural competencies when treating black people. Bailey provides some historical grounding for his readers, thereby giving some con-text for folk healing. However, the cultural distinctiveness of African American folk healing with its unique history and perspective are erased under a rubric of "alternative medicine." Like the Slave Narra-tives' use of Negro dialect, this current usage reduces African Ameri-can folk healing to something that mainstream culture wants to see in black culture.

Ishmael Reed uses a different, poetic definition of hoodoo that em-phasizes its spiritual dimension:

> Neo-HooDoo is a "Lost American Church" updated. . . . In Neo-Hoo-Doo, Christ the landlord deity ("render unto Caesar") is on proba-tion. . . . Whereas the center of Christianity lies the graveyard . . . and the cross. The center of Neo-HooDoo is the drum, the anhk and the Dance. . . . Neo-HooDoo is a litany seeking its text. . . . *You can't keep a good church down!*[8]

Reed's definition contrasts the spirituality of Christianity, centered on death, with that of hoodoo, centered on life and joy. His poetry cap-tures the spirit of many I interviewed, such as Renee, who said, "Hoo-doo is *mine.*" His creative approach to renaming hoodoo is a reminder of the processes of hybridization along with the search for the healing of black identities and religion.

In each of these redefinitions or reinterpretations of black folk healing, the continuing processes of hybridization are seen. If defining from within black perspectives, the history that black Americans have experienced is included; this means that something will change from the past. If interpreting across racial lines or to more popular audi-ences, the use of terms familiar to those audiences creates something a little different from the original healing practice. Each of these processes of defining or interpreting African American folk healing practices also demonstrates its continued influence in America.

Lessons from Hoodoo Class

In June 2004, I attended a hoodoo lesson that was offered in Detroit. This lesson, along with others, was offered as part of a series entitled "Hoodoo 101." Each lesson cost seventy-five dollars and lasted four hours. On the flyer announcing the classes were instructions: "Our Hoo Doo classes fill up fast and space is limited to 12 students. Register Early. Places are reserved with a $20 deposit. Herbs, oils and cloth bags are provided. Other magical items are available for purchase."

The lesson I attended taught the art of making mojo bags. Charms or amulets known as "mojos" or "hands" are used for healing or protection. The objective is to draw the desired result, such as love or luck. The person for whom it is intended may carry it, or the bag may be left in a place where it can work. Thus a mojo that is to bring about the sale of a house may be left near the entrance; a mojo that insures a person's health might be carried.

Everyday objects are used in the mojo bag: herbs found in the kitchen; stones easily purchased at nature shops; flowers from the garden. Each of these items is understood to have a power—to heal or to otherwise change present circumstance. Selected oils, animal parts (such as a chicken foot), or roots purchased at health food stores may be ingredients as well. The selection of what to use depends on the purpose for which the bag is being made. Some items are intended to make the bag more powerful: a feather brings about the desired event more rapidly or makes communication more effective. A mojo bag for the success of a journey may include a dollar with the imprint of the Native American Sacajawea; this smoothes the path of travel. Other elements that may be used are salt; nail or hair clippings; and dirt from a grave. Each item is understood to have special properties, and it is the role of the practitioner to know what to use, for what purpose, and in what combination.

The bag into which these items are placed is often part of the charm. The color of the cloth may have symbolic meaning, such as gold or green for prosperity. The teachers in the class I attended considered red flannel a traditional material to use; the flannel was recycled from family underwear. The bag should be closed and bound with twine or other thread that may have symbolism; it can also be sewn together by the maker.

After it is made, the bag should be blessed. The bag maker decides how to do this. For instance, our instructors stated that some people felt more comfortable praying for Jesus or God to bring forth power from the bag. Others might concentrate on the ingredients in the bag, particularly what they mean, and call forth their power. Ultimately, the bag holds symbolism and hopes and should not be handled by others. To have others handle the bag would weaken the mojo's power because the new element of another person's energy is added. The bag should then be regularly fed, at least once a week, with either oils or strong liquor. The feeding is a time that the maker concentrates again on the intent of the bag. After the purpose for which the bag was created is achieved, it should be carefully dismantled and contents such as herbs and flowers placed in the earth; stones and Sacajawea dollars should be retained for future use.

Another name for this type of charm is a nation bag. A nation bag is regional, found primarily in Tennessee, and has a slightly different purpose. Black women have traditionally had charge of their families' care, including finances. The nation bags have been used as charms to protect the family and hold some of the family's money. In other words, these women held the care of the "nation." The handling of the bag is particularly restricted; men should not touch the bag or its contents.

As we have seen, those who are attracted to contemporary folk healing have very different experiences from the black people of sixty or even thirty years ago. The students in the small class I attended were all women. Some were just curious; others were already involved in a form of traditional African religions of which this class felt like a natural extension. Both black women and white women took the class; the white women were likewise involved in traditional African religion or in Wicca. All the women I spoke with had a sense of spiritual expression in what they were doing; they generally seemed motivated to learn new ways to expresses their spirituality.

One of the teachers of the class was Renee, whom I later interviewed. The class began with a lecture by Renee about the African roots of black Americans. We pored over a map of Africa, discussing the main regions from which African Americans had been taken as well as the areas in the colonies where they had been sold. We also discussed the religions and spiritual practices of those areas of Africa from which most black Americans had been taken. In BaKongo culture, for instance, feathers represent communication and swiftness; hence they are used in a mojo bag to obtain a speedier result.

In this look at African cultures, Renee was careful to link the past of enslavement to current practices of hoodoo. She traced how enslaved Africans had saved their cultural perspectives and how those practices were shaped in the United States. Saint medals, for example, could be used in mojo bags and the custom permeated the New Orleans area of Catholic influence. So a medal of Saint Michael is used in these bags to draw protection; the Virgin Mary, to draw healing; Saint Martha, to dominate a male lover; or Mary Magdalene, to draw love.

All women taking the class were working; some were more comfortably middle class than others. For instance, one African American woman owns her own business. All of the women had some college education. At least three of the women with whom I spoke, including Renee, are involved in some of the fine arts. Their educational levels and status reinforce our earlier discussions about the relationships of class and the retention of black culture.

There was a long discussion in the class about using hoodoo offensively, which is "throwing" a spell with negative results on another person in a preemptive strike. This topic elicited strong feelings from most of the participants concerning persons who have harmed or intend to cause harm: what would the spiritual consequences be for the person using power with intent to cause harm? The importance of self-care—including self-protection—as a sign of self-esteem indicated emotional health and spiritual maturity for the participants. Self-protection was contrasted with Christian "turn the other cheek" teachings because the other cheek often results in the most socially vulnerable being harmed the most, as African American experience attests. "Fixing" the situation through magic before severe damage is done is not considered evil; the real evil, most concurred, is to simply accept whatever is happening.

Further discussions concerned the ethical foundation of hoodoo. There is no explicit moral code listing behavioral regulations that, if transgressed, have defined penalties. The persons who seek help and the persons who provide it share responsibility for whatever work is attempted and its results. Practitioners are expected to think, acting from interdependent relationships, and then choose on behalf of the greater good. To harm without cause would have negative consequences, but even the penalties that result can be corrected. All aspects of "fixing" someone are within the realm of healing work broadly conceived, by preventing harm and correcting situations. These ideas constitute an ethical stance within hoodoo that calls forth personal responsibility with mutuality.

I attended one lesson that was clearly a demonstration of how African Americans are reclaiming hoodoo concepts and practices. The deliberate focus on black culture included distinguishing between African-derived and white value systems. Discussions of ethics and self-protections, for instance, set out historical considerations for decision making; discussions of herbs and stones imply intimate relationships between humans, nature, and the Divine. These conversations among the students who attended the class seemed to affirm the ideas they had upon entering. In other words, attending the sessions is a matter of choice; those who do not have similar conceptions would likely choose not to participate.

Processes of hybridization were being performed in these classes as students and teachers drew multiple traditions, from Santería to Wicca to Christianity, into dialogue during their construction of mojo bags. Hoodoo seemed to assist students' clarification about what they want out of life or from a given situation. This could be seen as the teachers worked individually with students to select the ingredients in the right combinations to go into the mojo bags that would address their individual situations. Hoodoo served an integrating function for participants to draw together aspects of culture, their ideas of the supernatural, and their own experiences. Some comments indicated this function: "I always wondered why black people did that," or "I always felt that way too."

Conjurers of the past may have used informal apprenticeships to teach aspirants, but in these classes, hoodoo is taught by using the methods of this era. Classes were advertised by flyer. Students could pay by check. Sessions were held on Saturday to accommodate work and worship schedules. The teachers showed that magic could be performed with herbs that can be in any kitchen. They presented hoodoo as both rational and accessible for twenty-first-century practitioners.

Conjuring Work

I interviewed two women who practice hoodoo. One of them is Renee, who led the discussion about questions of ethics and morality in hoodoo. A portion of her interview is in the preceding chapter. The perceived absence of an ethical perspective in hoodoo among many not familiar with its workings is often extended in such a way that all black people are negatively defined as amoral. Renee suspected that some hoodoo practitioners today add to the image of amoral black people through their cleavage of their work from traditional African worldviews. "When you take the spells from the context, as some have, it appears that African Americans don't have ethics guiding what they do."

There is honesty in hoodoo for Renee because it retains African culture. "Hoodoo came about because there were no saints to hide it behind [as in Catholicism]. They [the enslaved black people] adapted with what they had." This same creativity and spirituality can be seen in the spirituals and the blues. The connection with Africa is important to Renee; it is a source of pride. She looks at hoodoo and African religious belief systems in comparison with European systems that aim to tap into the energies of the universe. "Africans [Egyptians, Sumerians] did it before the Europeans *and* wrote it down."

She initially thought about starting hoodoo classes when she found Web sites that offered online information, complete with certification. Renee was convinced that her classes must include a component on Africa and the slave trade in order to provide the context for hoodoo. She also felt that sessions should aim for quality rather than sensationalism.

In February 2005, I also interviewed Jackie, the owner of a candle shop in the Detroit area. Candle production and sales, like Jackie's, are as easy to find as books about hoodoo. The candles are used for multiple purposes. Some have intentions written on them; as the candles burn, the intention is fulfilled. The intentions include any desired outcome, such as health, protection, or keeping in-laws away. Candles are also used ritually, such as using their smoke for purification of an object or a person. Most hoodoo candle shops are found in urban neighborhoods. They are often small storefronts, known to the neighborhood, with nonexistent budgets for advertising. Floor washes, candles, incenses, powders, spiritual baths, and other products for the practice of hoodoo are found among their inventories. As mentioned in an earlier chapter, from the 1930s to the present, candle stores have been important avenues for continuing black folk healing practices. The stores are discussed more fully later in this chapter.

Jackie shared many of the same ideas as Renee about hoodoo. Yet, Jackie's involvement was different; not only is she the owner of a candle shop, she is white. She manufactures several lines of products, among them, Motor City Hoodoo. When I asked how she got into hoodoo, she mentioned books she had read on the subject. However, she has been working with "magic since high school. I was brought up Catholic. I always wanted to be religious and spiritual, but I was not able to find it in the Catholic Church." Around the age of eighteen, she found a book on dream interpretation, "and that was my beginning in Wicca." Jackie has since been involved in magical practices from around the world, and through these explorations, found traditional African religion and hoodoo.

"The way I've used herbs," Jackie remarked, "has been more of the African traditions rather than the European. I found my rhythm with hoodoo. It's what I've been doing all along." I asked pointedly about her being a white woman working with hoodoo. "It doesn't bother me I'm white. You have to recognize where hoodoo comes from, and not make it white." Recognition of hoodoo's African and slavery roots means that there must be respect for those who came before, and "not belittle who they were. I feel like I'm getting back to the core, because all life comes from Africa." Jackie dislikes that other religions or writers incorporate hoodoo without the African context; she finds that doing so misrepresents the practices.

Jackie defined what makes hoodoo different from other supernatural traditions: "In hoodoo, the secret sauce is the spirit. The spirit" is elemental. The spirit is the energy in all things, it's "some of the energy of creation, and you're asking for a piece of that" in hoodoo spells. We humans should not try to understand the logic behind the workings of the spirits because "[we] can't think the way they think." In hoodoo, the spirit is "food, communication, and story, and you tap into that primal energy." Jackie has seen a difference in the Motor City hoodoo line of products and an earlier line she produced of blessed herbal candles. The blessed herbal candles would bring change, but the hoodoo line brings the magic in, and "you have to decide what to do with it. The elemental spirits are neutral. Elemental spirits *are* the secret sauce."

Jackie explained that this approach to the supernatural is different from processes of putting a piece of yourself into magic, as in other traditions. "When you pray [in those traditions, such as Wicca], you pray from the heart, you pray with a piece of yourself, and you can break in half in the process." The elemental spirits called on—"whatever you call it, whether it's God-source energy, whatever"—in hoodoo are outside the self.

She noted that some stores carrying the Motor City Hoodoo line come back repeatedly for supplies. The steady customers say that the candles and hoodoo bags work faster. Jackie believes that these products work faster because they go to the core of the person and set up change. Yet there are other stores that refuse to carry the products. They refuse because "I don't want voodoo in my place."

Jackie related some of her encounters with people who come to her for products. She gets calls for consultations in three main areas: money ("What am I supposed to do about my finances?"); crossed conditions (or people who believe they have had a curse placed on them); and love ("How do I make him love me?"). For instance, a woman was opening a second restaurant and needed more money. So, after consulting with Jackie, she lit one of the blessed candles in her restaurant. Later a man came into the restaurant and told her, "I love this place." The woman seeking money asked him, "Do you want to invest?" He did, and so she was able to open her next restaurant.

The interviews with these two conjuring women underscore several ideas that have been discussed throughout this book. The routes that bring people to hoodoo, conjure, and folk healing are not as they had been in the past. A chance discovery of a book or involvement with other religions might lead to a rediscovery of hoodoo. Unlike the situation of the people interviewed in the Slave Narratives, there is no explicit sense of hoodoo or folk healing being "everywhere."

Both Jackie and Renee talked about finding a spiritual home in hoodoo. With Renee, cultural pride and ownership were evident in her comments. Jackie was able to identify a point of human connection ("It's what I've been doing all along") as a way to claim hoodoo, even as she named the African origins. Both women followed a spiritual path of discovery to hoodoo. In this journey, they were also like Ann and Sokara and Mahdi and others interviewed. The development of their spiritual lives took them outside mainstream constructions; their approaches to sorting and rearranging information participate in hybridizing forms of religions and cultures.

Jackie's interview illustrates several connections. One of the Slave Narratives interviewees had discussed white folks who would sneak to get black folk treatments. The exchange between white and black Americans has often involved this back door approach; when white people adopt black life styles, they may be called traitors to their race. Jackie is white and treads respectfully into black culture. She asserts that white participants in hoodoo should not make it "white." In this, she refers to patterns of cultural dominance that often occur when white people appropriate black culture. At the same time, Jackie is an entrepreneur, selling products based on black culture. It is significant that Jackie is concerned with maintaining the connection of hoodoo to Africa and black enslavement. She is deliberate in her decision to not make hoodoo "white." Jackie's contacts with black people are not merely what she has gleaned from books, but through interaction. She is willing to listen and learn in her interactions with black people, while not forcing her interpretations on black activities or ideas. This dynamic has generally not been in evidence in the history of black people in conversation with white Americans. That history is continued in some aspects of the commercialization of hoodoo.

Selling Hoodoo

Folk healing is integral to hoodoo. Those who seek hoodoo products are seeking wholeness of body, mind, spirit, emotions, finances, and living situations. Such wholeness may be defined as social power or a better home; seeking it is a spiritual quest.

The hoodoo class and Jackie's line of hoodoo products are aspects of hoodoo in the marketplace. The hoodoo class I attended may be unique for some areas. However, there are other ways that people who are interested can gather information. Popular books are readily available that detail hoodoo and related spell work, such as Tayannah McQuillar's *Rootwork*. Another example is Stephanie Rose Bird's *Sticks, Stones, Roots and Bones* hoodoo. Like McQuillar, she presents ingredients and spells. As a point of comparison, Bird defines hoodoo as an American tradition that is not a religion but "primarily healing traditions that involve the use of herbs, plants, roots, trees, animals, magnets, minerals, and natural waters combined with magical amulets, chants, ceremonies, rituals, and handmade power objects."[9] The other tradition mentioned in this definition that she puts in the same category as hoodoo is Candomblé. But her information here is incorrect, because Candomblé is a religion, not merely a healing tradition.

Bird presents background information on the different charms and spell for which she lists recipes. For instance, she instructs the reader to chant certain words when preparing a given spell and explains:

> Why? Speaking directly to the pot, fire, candle, and herb is essential. Remember, Hoodoo has strong roots in African animistic philosophy. Animistic philosophy considers each element or aspect of nature as being alive. Natural objects . . . have a universal energy force within them to which we are all connected. To simply use herbs, flowers, stones, bones, fire, or water without paying homage to its life force insults the spirits.[10]

Clarity based on history and African traditional religions is missing from this definition about what it means to consider aspects of nature in connection with humans. Therefore, Bird misses the holistic connections of nature with humans with the Divine; the uses of the natural objects in her book become magic tricks. By missing these holistic interconnections, Bird does not really define black religious thinking.

Bird liberally sprinkles her book with aspects of astrology and various religions, particularly various deities, mentioning that they are a "multicultural selection of goddesses and gods."[11] She creatively builds her own version of hoodoo, similar to the creative approach of Sokara and her healing practice. At the same time, Bird states that hoodoo is not a religion.[12] Unlike Sokara, Bird is not situated within an African American context. In spite of the artificiality of Bird's use of multicultural deities, this is still a form of hybridization. The difficulty with her approach is that black cultural reference points are lost or made into trends, leading into the commercialization that Renee predicted.

Another book that is widely used is Catherine Yronwode's *Hoodoo Herb and Root Magic*. Yronwode, who is white, states in the introduction that she is indebted to "teachers, friends, and customers in the

African American community." Her approach to her subject, like Jackie's, is a very long way from Louise Oliphant and the Slave Narratives in the 1930s; whiteness is not a sociopolitical barrier to understanding another culture as it was then. Yronwode says of the purpose of her book:

> My attempt to give something of value back to the community that has given me so much. It is a hoodoo grimoire or conjure doctor's spell book, first and foremost, but it is also a teaching tool designed to give today's root workers a basic botanical vocabulary, so that they won't be tricked by unscrupulous suppliers any more.[13]

A basic book to prevent rootworkers from being tricked, Yronwode states, is necessary because in the 1970s, some of the merchants of herbs began to switch plants that had been ordered:

> A policy that was once explained to me as "substituting green for green and brown for brown" or "making six herbs sell like a dozen." In short, with the exception of plants that had visually distinctive leaves (like Rosemary) or an unmistakable aroma (like Mint), these suppliers felt free to substitute any cut and sifted herb for another of similar appearance.[14]

Her book includes drawings and descriptions of plants as well as hoodoo uses. Overall, it is a well-researched text of this type. Her audience, as she states, is practitioners, so she may feel a need to take more caution than Bird, who is addressing a different audience.

In addition to books, candle stores communicate ideas about folk healing while they help sell the products. Additionally people learn how to locate the stores with the items they want for their practice of hoodoo or healing. Carolyn Long discussed how she found the stores for her study:

> There are hundreds, maybe even thousands, of spiritual stores in the United States, located in cities and small towns with large African American or Latino populations. The number and orientation of these merchants in any given locale depends primarily on demographics. . . . [L]ooking under "religious goods" or "candles" in the yellow pages . . . candle shops, , botánicas, and yerberías are listed

along with the Christian bookstores, church supply houses, Hebrew gift shops, and New Age boutiques—the purveyors of Bibles and prayer books, choir robes, rosaries and holy cards, yarmulkes and menorahs, crystals and herbal essences.[15]

Some candle stores are directly associated with a church. For instance, in Detroit, I found Reverend Matthews's brightly painted candle store and church (see photo at beginning of chapter). The small church and store are connected. The store had items for sale, including blessed elephants and blessed thinking caps. Most of the items seemed home made, rather than ordered from a commercial line of products. In this store, I encountered people resistant to speaking with me at all; this was not my experience in any of the other stores I visited. In fact, most other people were eager to enter into conversations about what they used and why.

Another candle store in Detroit is Discount Candles. When I visited, the white proprietor was behind the counter blending special oils and dressing (applying oil and herbs for greater effectiveness) votive candles for her customers' particular needs. There are shelves with already-dressed candles, but one customer mentioned that it's best to have the candle dressed "fresh." A Spanish-speaking woman worker in the store tried to steer customers toward Santería product lines. The all-black clientele bypassed her and went to the proprietor for consultations. Such consultations could be for spiritual needs, physical health, or to draw love, luck, or money. All the stores I visited had a person who was available for advising customers about the products and suggesting which one would be more effective. I have overheard such an advisor directing a client to take more of an herb or to continue some form of treatment.

The clientele at Discount Candles on the day I visited knew what they sought, although they occasionally asked if one product were more effective than another. Sometimes, the conversations about choice products were between the counter staff and customer, sometimes among customers. The customers and staff formed a kind of community that included other candle stores. Several informed me about problems with another store, one that used to be up the street. It seems that there had been a competition between the two stores. The proprietor was also able to tell me the locations of other candle stores along with information about the owners' lives.

Candle stores are easy to locate and their continuation in black communities are evidence of a spiritual search for wholeness. Like any kind of business, there are some shops that are more respected than others. Luisah Teish, a priestess in Lucumí, recounts her visit to a candle shop:

> I stop in another candle shop in downtown New Orleans. . . . There are about fifty brand-name candles burning on the counter. I see Uncrossing, Black Cat, Fast Luck, Lucky Dream, Money, Money Drawing, Money Luck, Fast Money Luck, Lucky Hand, Helping Hand, Go Way Evil, *ad nauseam*. . . . "I specialize in gambling hands," the woman tells me, "You want a gambling hand?" Taking the barrenness of the place as evidence, I conclude that this shop is no more than a front for a numbers runner.[16]

As Teish demonstrates, there are African Americans who do not believe in candle shops.

Not all stores are owned and operated by black or white Americans; some are operated by and from the perspectives of people from other countries. Their religious views are still derivatives of African traditional religions. They bring Santería, Lucumí, and other forms of Yoruban religion directly to the United States. Their stores and communities provide new levels of cultural education to, and exchange with, black people in the United States that can result in changes to black religious practice. As Carolyn Long stated, cross-fertilization has occurred: "The customers of candle shops, botánicas, and yerberías are reinterpreting and adapting the products for their own uses. Some black Americans who come out [of] a hoodoo tradition are buying the accoutrements of the orichas. Latinos are buying John the Conqueror roots and products."[17] There will be changes spurred by the exchanges among different traditions. Meanwhile, another change in hoodoo is the result of the technology of the computer age.

On the Internet

Hoodoo sites, information, and products are available on the Internet. For example, some items like oils and candles can be purchased on eBay. There are also Web sites devoted to promoting hoodoo. Some of the sites are simply marketplaces for products, like Grandma Rosa's Dreamstone Gallery, which is little more than an online candle store.[18] The products offered include oils, incense, jewelry, soaps, and some spell kits. There is no philosophy or spirituality being offered at Grandma Rose's, except for one quotation: "Everything I do is to feed YOUR spirit, make YOU powerful . . . and help YOU get what YOU desire." The heavily emphasized "you" is clearly a marketing ploy—getting the potential customer to feel cared about and engaged by the site. The lack of ability to build community and to engage face-to-face is one of the limits of the Internet; this is a problem for an online candle store that cannot provide the personal attention to customers that was experienced at Discount Candle. However, if a person does not live near one of the candle stores, the Internet, even a site like this one, would be welcome to the hoodoo practitioner.

But there are Web sites that find ways to engage customers. These become sources for more intensive information about hoodoo, but they can also provide varied or contested viewpoints of what conjure entails. Such sites often offer different definitions of hoodoo. Catherine Yronwode, mentioned above, defines hoodoo as African American folk magic on her Web site:

> Like folk magic of many other cultures, hoodoo attributes magical properties to herbs, toots, minerals (especially the lodestone), animal parts, and the personal possessions and bodily effluvia of people. the African origins of hoodoo can clearly be seen in such non-European magical customs as jinxing, hot footing, foot track magic, crossing and crossroads magic, in which are embedded remnants of the folkloric beliefs of the Yoruba, Fon, Ewe, and Congo people.[19]

Yronwode is white, and some of my informants complained that she is one who takes hoodoo out of context. Yet, some of her explanations were clear and grounded in African belief systems. She offers an online hoodoo correspondence course[20] with a certificate awarded upon completion and also has a radio show. Not surprisingly, each of the Web pages points back to her Lucky Mojo Curio Occult shop.

Another Web site presents hoodoo differently. The Mami Wata Healers Society of North America is a religious movement that connects black American religious thought with African roots. Mama Zogbé, one of the leaders of the group, defined hoodoo on her Web site as an "an African mystical tradition, known by various names, that is practiced all over Africa, and has been for thousands of years. It is perhaps the first tangible application of the supernatural."[21] Hoodoo is not magic as she defines it. She mentions the use of herbs and amulets but relates each with African practices. She distinguishes a rootworker as an herbalist and a conjurer as someone who works more with the practices of hoodoo. Mama Zogbé's definition structures her religion's theology around African values.

Hoodoo is still in the United States, but changes are occurring in it. The Internet and African Diaspora cultures will have influences. Popularizing books are available in the chain bookstores, and this will introduce new people to hoodoo. From these popularized versions of hoodoo, changes will certainly occur. Therefore, the descriptions above should be considered a snapshot of current practices and discussions around hoodoo that will stand in comparison to future changes.

With the Spirit

So far, we have observed African American folk healing in terms of the physical world. But in what ways does folk healing still deal with the spirit world?

The spiritual is related to healing in the physical world in several ways. The African American folk healing mindset considers all life as interconnected and hence one part of life is able to influence another. The influence results in energy for healing that can be accessed by the person who has the knowledge. A black midwife who practiced in Alabama from the 1930s to the late 1970s who talked about having performed mouth-to-mouth resuscitation on an infant was asked who had taught her how. She replied, "No ma'am I hadn't been taught how to do that. I progressed that outa my mind. My own mind. There was a higher power and God give me wisdom. Motherwit, common sense. Wisdom come from on high."[22] These types of other-imparted knowledge of how to perform a healing action are common. Ann, who is interviewed in chapter 4, speaks about how her spirit guides give her information about healing. This source of information outside oneself communicates directly to those who listen. This idea was also verbalized by the faith healers Evangelists Earma and Cleopatra, and in their case, the information on and power for healing came directly from God. The interconnections of spiritual and physical are more like two sides of the same coin of life in African American folk healing conceptualizations.

During hoodoo class, Renee told the participants of two BaKongo beliefs that are related to elements used in mojo bags. In one, "earth from a grave is at one with the spirit of the person buried in it." This "goofer dust," as it is called in African American hoodoo, is used because it is can make the mojo bag extremely potent. In the second belief, a cross with equal arms stands for the "four moments of the Sun in Kongo theology, representing the eternal movement of the human spirit through the worlds of the living and the dead."[23]

Interpreting signs is a basic way that an African American folk healing mindset reflects on interactions of the human/physical and the spirit world. Signs can be considered from God, deceased relatives, angels, or nature. Determining what a sign is, such as a particular bird or rain, is not formulaic and is individualized for each person based on what is happening in his or her life. Signs are not like traffic directions, clear and to the point. Instead, they need the imagination of the person to see them and then some time will be required to recognize them as signs that have meaning for that person.

Dreams are also ways of getting messages from the spirit world. Deceased relatives bearing messages or the signs that hold meaning for a certain message. Dreams may direct one's future path by giving warnings about the inadvisability of a career or by pointing to new possibilities. Dream books are often in candle stores, and these interpret the meanings of dreams as signs of winning lottery numbers. In many black neighborhoods, small stores with lottery machines will sell dream books, and these are displayed near the lottery machines. Stories that tell of people's getting messages or signs that warned against marriage or led to lottery winnings are often told among African Americans.

Death is inescapable and, with a folk healing mindset, not a final break with life. This mindset is seen at many African American funerals that are sometimes called "Home Going Celebrations." Additionally, there is a common belief that those who have been dead less than three days (or other specified time) sometimes visit one of the remaining family members, often to bring comfort.

Stephanie Bird describes several death-related charms in her book.

Some commemorate the deceased, such as "release incense" and "lift me up pine floor wash."[24] One is specific to those who survive: a grief bag that can be offered to mourners at a funeral.[25]

Other practices related to dealing with death may be specific to families. An elderly aunt of mine once called upon me to make the decision to attend the funeral of a distant family member. "After all," she said, "this is the last time you'll be able to go to church with him." The notions that the man would be present at his funeral or that attendees would be *with* him at the event also calls attention to African American sense of the connections between life and death. That my elderly aunt was the one to call me to attend to my familial duty highlights another feature of black cultural practice.

My elderly aunt was the one in the family who knew everybody, knew the history, and could call upon any member to fulfill some duty. Someone in black families has borne the responsibility to remember the past or call the other members to task. Most often, I have heard of the role's being filled by one of the elderly women in a family. This informal, culturally based practice affirmed the importance of the elderly; when instructed to do something, the only choice was to comply. This sense of honoring the elderly is related to the idea of honoring the ancestors, those who have gone before and, as the saying goes, on whose shoulders we stand. The role of the family matriarch or patriarch seems to be lessening as black families have become more geographically spread out. However, the sense of honoring ancestors continues and is captured in black family reunions.

Briefly, to recap, some of the ways that hoodoo and other aspects of folk healing are expressed in American cultural life today have included the sale of books and candles, in shops and through the Internet; definitions related to hoodoo that are used today; and the ways in which the spiritual and physical worlds are seen as connected in a folk healing mindset. Each of these is an expression of African American folk healing today; each demonstrates the changes that have occurred even as hybridization is continuing. But the future of black folk healing is not at all clear.

Conclusion

I do Reiki, I do the mind-body integration and the whole brainwork, and I do the color therapy . . . and flower essences. . . . And I use gemstones, and crystals and crystal elixirs. I use some vibrational work related to the ancestors. That's very African and Native American based, but [what] I'm doing is a kind of new form that I got in a dream state from my ancestors. . . . One thing that I did say, even when I was 5 or 6 years old, is that God has been everywhere on the planet and has given a message to all people. And all of those messages are correct, nobody has a patent on the truth. And Jesus didn't get everywhere, and God is not that limited.

—Sokara, interview with author

This book has considered various aspects of the fully American story of African American folk healing. Through slavery and Jim Crow, black bodies were socially constructed in negative frameworks to justify their oppression. Black Americans countered this dehumanization with other constructions drawn from a cultural base that retains African cognitive orientation. Thus, the social construction of black bodies has overlapped with the cultural constructions of health and wellness. Throughout this exploration, we have seen how African Americans have interacted with white and Native Americans, and we have seen the processes of hybridity writ large as African Americans have used healing to counter negative American images.

Many of the voices and views we have encountered are often unseen or misunderstood in the wider American cultural landscape. The misunderstandings become part of the story as African Americans interact with oppression and respond to their marginalized status through concepts of wellness that are grounded in holistic views of the human person. To intentionally break that holistic framework—as white slave owners and racists have done—was believed by black people to result in serious physical, mental, and spiritual consequences, such as a tragic death or debilitating illness. White Americans, meanwhile, have seldom been aware of the ways *they* are judged and *their* bodies read by black Americans. This is one example of the chasm between black and white Americans that has facilitated mutual misunderstandings. The sociocultural gaps that segregated African Americans from whites conversely created spaces where black cultural forms such as folk healing could continue.

However, these counterconstructions of identity and wellness, even based on long-standing African cognitive orientations, can be dangerous. Most of the people I interviewed continued in a state of health throughout my writing of this book, but one woman, committed to using folk methods *solely*, died, in her fifties. Whether she died of the illness that she used folk healing to treat is unknown to me. Her probably avoidable demise is a tragedy that may lead some to condemn folk practices, yet many African Americans have died in equally tragic ways while under the care of institutional medicine. Simply put, numerous African Americans continue, with cause, to demonstrate a lack of trust of institutional medicine.

I once accompanied an elderly black woman to her first chemotherapy treatment for cancer. The attending nurse, also black, asked the patient, "Do you know why you are here?" I was stunned by the question. After the patient interview was over, I queried the nurse about why she had posed it. She responded that because many African Americans are referred to other places by their medical doctors without also being informed of their diagnosis or treatment plan, she has learned to ask whether they have been given this information. Oftentimes she becomes the one who informs the patient about his or her state of health. This story highlights the ongoing difficulties facing African Americans as they contend with institutional medicine. Of course, many people of all races are uncertain how to access services, even if they have some form of medical insurance, but this may be particularly so for members of the African American community. Greater cultural competence is the sine qua non in resolving the cultural gaps between African Americans' and institutional medicine's sometimes oppositional cultures.

This story contrasts with the feeling of satisfaction reported by the woman who later died. She was happy and comforted in her choices for healing work, trustful of black folkways healers. As we saw in the reports from the Folk Archives, she saw actual results from folk methods. Her approach in using solely black folk healing, though, differs from the approaches of many other people I interviewed who had no problem with using *any* form of healing—institutional or folk medicine or some combination—to achieve wellness.

While closing the cultural gaps is necessary for institutional medicine to work more closely with African American communities, it should not be assumed that success in closing the gaps would or should terminate the existence of black folk healing. African American folk healing developed from the base of the culture, not merely necessity. Black folk healing is one way African Americans make sense of the world. It reflects the central tenet of a holistic view of the human person in community connected with nature. Black folk healing indicates how, culturally, African Americans act as agents in defining their own bodies, exerting some control over life, and constructing identity. Thinking of black folk healing in this way may help to explain why my twenty-something college-educated daughter still takes care with the disposal of her cut hair: she seeks understanding of what it means to be black in America, which, more than a political project, is also a spiritual undertaking.

African American folk healing continues to change and evolve, as we have seen. Through this book we have developed a clearer picture than commonly understood of African Americans whose searches for meaning are framed by experiences of marginalization and of the layered meanings of African American folk healing that have evolved over time, bringing new dimensions to life. Changes in folk healing have been necessarily traced through relevant history, as black people brought their African cognitive orientations into new situations. The Slave Narratives of the 1930s and the Folk Archives accounts of the 1970s are important markers of developments across the twentieth century. Our consideration of folk healing's cultural groundings has illuminated its epistemological foundations, including processes of hybridization. The theological foundations of black religion are intimated in discussions around a black mystical tradition and other issues of spirituality. We have considered contested aspects of black culture, including how language shapes black Americans and healing practices. And we have seen how African American views of wellness and illness contrast with the culture of institutional medicine. These basic concepts have been illuminated by interviews with Americans who now practice some form of black folk healing.

African American folk healing, with its aims of balancing relationships and renewing life, has provided a haven for cultural and intellectual development. Yet as we have seen, all of these aspects are being challenged by current commercial ventures, on the Internet and in bookstores, that focus on black folk healing and make it into a commodity.

African American folk healing is in dialogue with other American cultures and traditions; new forms of commerce impact it; and alternative medicines influence it. At the same time, black folk healing maintains a global dimension. African people throughout the Diaspora are entering into new forms of dialogue as globalization continues and necessarily engenders further changes to folk healing. We have seen how wider networks of communication and cultural exchange have made an impact in several ways, such as candle stores in black communities that may sell candles to various orishas of Cuban-derived Santería or African Americans who practice African traditional religions. As diverse, complex, and layered as these global cultural patterns may be, they also conversely underscore the importance of black culture. They serve to reiterate that African American folk healing continues to flow from the base of culture (no matter how slippery), embedded in wider cultural patterns that ultimately enliven black communities.

African American approaches to the body, wellness, and healing are deeply linked to expressions of spirituality and faith. The quote from Sokara demonstrates the wide exchanges across cultures—reflected in the various healing modalities she uses—even as she interprets them in an African Americanized frame of reference. She participates in and shapes aspects of black culture within black communities. Through her words it is apparent that she uses her healing work as grounding to challenge forms of Christianity that construct religion as an exercise in exclusivity.

Sokara's challenge brings us back to the central dimension of black folk healing. At its heart, African American folk healing reflects a spirituality of healing. Although it may be manifest in large ways in African American culture—such as faith healing—and in other ways in political life—such as the Maafa event—this spirituality is shown as well in myriad ways in everyday experiences. This spirituality of healing helps African Americans to envision new lives for themselves and to dream of new futures for the country. It is the difference, I believe, between a people merely surviving and one finding ways to transcend centuries of racial oppression.

Notes

Notes to Chapter I

1. Bernice Bowden interviewer, http://memory.loc/gov/mss/mesn/023/252251.tif.

2. Zora Neale Hurston, *Go Gator and Muddy the Waters: Writings by Zora Neale Hurston from the Federal Writers' Project* (New York: W. W. Norton, 1999).

3. Louise Oliphant, "Work, Play, Food, Clothing, Marriage, etc.," Compilation Richmond County Ex-Slave Interviews, Library of Congress, Manuscript Division, http://memory.loc.gov/mss/mesn/044/359355.gif, October 2004.

4. Louise Oliphant, "Mistreatment of Slaves," Library of Congress, Manuscript Division, http://memory.loc.gov/mss/mesn/044/295291.gif, October 2004.

5. M. B. Stonestreet, interview of Adeline Willis, vol. 4, part 4, WPA Slave Narrative Project, WPA Manuscript Division, Library of Congress, http://memory.loc.gov/mss/mesn/044/165161.tif.

6. Louise Oliphant, "Conjuration," http://memory.loc.gov/mss/mesn/044/273269.gif, October 2004.

7. Louise Oliphant, "Folk Remedies and Superstitions," Compilation Folklore Interviews—Richmond County, Georgia, Library of Congress, Manuscript Division, http://memory.loc.gov/mss/mesn/044/286282.gif, October 2004.

8. Ibid., http://memory.loc.gov/mss/mesn/044/289285.gif, October 2004.

9. Ibid., http://memory.loc,gov/mss/mesn/044/288284.gif, October 2004.

10. Ibid., http://memory.loc.gov/mss/mesn/044/290286.gif, October 2004.

11. Amanda McDaniel, interviewed by Edwin Driskell, WPA Slave Narrative Project, Georgia Narratives, http://memory.loc.gov/mss/mesn/043/074071.tif.

12. Bryant Huff, interviewed by Adella S. Dixon, WPA Slave Narrative Project, Georgia Narratives, http://memory.loc.gov/mss/mesn/042/241238.tif, October 2004.

13. Mr. Leonard, cited in WPA Slave Narrative Project, Georgia Narratives, http://memory.loc.gov/mss/mesn/044/265261.gif, November 2002.

14. WPA Slave Narrative Project, Georgia Narratives, http://memory.loc .gov/mss/mesn/044/267263.gif, November 2002.

15. Mr. Strickland, cited in WPA Slave Narrative Project, Georgia Narratives, http://memory.loc.gov/mss/mesn/044/266262.gif, November 2002.

16. WPA Slave Narrative Project, Georgia Narratives, http://memory.loc .gov/mss/mesn/044/268264.gif, November 2002.

17. Ibid.

18. WPA Slave Narrative Project, Georgia Narratives, http://memory.loc .gov/mss/mesn/044/271267.gif, November 2002.

19. Ibid.

20. Yvonne P. Chireau, *Religion and the African American Conjuring Tradition* (Berkeley: University of California Press, 2003), 4.

21. Sterling Stuckey, *Slave Culture: Nationalist Theory and the Foundations of Black America* (New York: Oxford University Press, 1987), 87.

22. Ibid., 91.

23. Ruth Bass, "Mojo" in *Mother Wit from the Laughing Barrel: Readings in the Interpretation of Afro-American Folklore*, edited by Alan Dundes (Englewood Cliffs, NJ: Prentice-Hall, 1973), 381.

24. WPA Slave Narrative Project, Georgia Narratives, Library of Congress, Manuscript Division, http://memory.loc.gov/mss/mesn/044/266262 .gif, November 2002.

25. Zora Neale Hurston, *The Sanctified Church* (Berkeley, CA: Turtle Island Press, 1981), 30–40.

26. Eugene D. Genovese, *Roll Jordan Roll: The World the Slaves Made* (New York: Vintage Books, 1976), 223.

27. Leonora Herron and Alice M. Bacon, "Conjuring and Conjure Doctors," in *Mother Wit from the Laughing Barrel: Readings in the Interpretation of Afro-American Folklore*, edited by Alan Dundes (Englewood Cliffs, NJ: Prentice-Hall, 1973), 361.

28. Deborah Gray White, *Ar'n't I a Woman? Female Slaves in the Plantation South* (New York: W. W. Norton, 1985), 115–16.

29. Martia Graham Goodson, "Medical-Botanical Contributions of African Slave Women to American Medicine," in *Black Women in American History*, edited by Darlene Clark Hine (New York: Carlson Publishing, 1990), 2.

30. Onnie Lee Logan, *Motherwit: An Alabama Midwife's Story* (New York: Plume Books, 1991), 63.

31. Arthur Huff Fauset, *Black Gods of the Metropolis: Negro Religious Cults of the Urban North*, vol. 3, Brinton Memorial Series (Philadelphia Anthropological Society, 1944; reprint University of Pennsylvania Press, 1971), 77–78. Father Divine began his Peace Mission in New York, and Bishop "Daddy" Grace, in Philadelphia and New York in the 1930s.

32. William Bascom, "Folklore," in *International Encyclopedia of the Social*

Sciences (1968), 196–97, cited in Bascom, "Folklore and the Africanist," *Journal of American Folklore*, vol. 86, no. 341 (July–September, 1973), 254.

33. Jerrilyn M. McGregory, *"There Are Other Ways to Get Happy" African-American Urban Folklore* (Ann Arbor: University of Michigan Press, 1992), 200.

34 Laura C. Jarmon, *Wishbone: Reference and Interpretation in Black Folk Narrative* (Knoxville: University of Tennessee Press, 2003), 320.

35. See also Loudell F. Snow, " 'I Was Born Just Exactly with the Gift': An Interview with a Voodoo Practitioner," *Journal of American Folklore*, vol. 86, no. 341 (July–September, 1973), 273–81.

36. Oliphant, "Conjuration," http://memory.loc.gov/mss/mesn/044/280276.gif, October 2004.

37. Ibid., http://memory.loc.gov/mss/mesn/044/283279.gif, October 2004.

38. Lee H. Butler Jr., "The Unpopular Experience of Popular Culture: Cultural Resistance as Identity Formation," *Journal of Pastoral Theology*, June 2001, 50.

39. Patricia J. Williams, "The Ethnic Scarring of American Whiteness," in *The House That Race Built: Black Americans, U.S. Terrain*, edited by Wahneema Lubiano (New York: Pantheon Books, 1997), 258.

40. David G. Holmes, *Revisiting Racialized Voice: African American Ethos in Language and Literature* (Carbondale: Southern Illinois University Press, 2004), 28, 29.

41. Houston A. Baker Jr., *Modernism and the Harlem Renaissance* (Chicago: University of Chicago Press, 1987), 21.

42. E. D. Hirsch Jr., *Cultural Literacy: What Every American Needs to Know* (New York: Vintage Books, 1988).

43. Hirsch's work is part of what is called by Catherine Prendergast the ideology of literacy, "the flawed but rhetorically seductive and seemingly deathless argument that literacy will guarantee equality of opportunity, moral growth, and financial security and ensure the democratic participation of all individuals in society, regardless of other factors." Catherine Prendergast, *Literacy and Racial Justice: The Politics of Learning after* Brown v. Board of Education (Carbondale: Southern Illinois University Press, 2003), 4.

44. Evelyn Brooks Higginbotham, "Rethinking Vernacular Culture: Black Religion and Race Records in the 1920s and 1930s," in *The House That Race Built: Black Americans, U.S. Terrain*, edited by Wahneema Lubiano (New York: Pantheon Books, 1997), 164.

45. Ibid., 159.

46. Ibid., 157–58.

47. David G. Nicholls, *Conjuring the Folk: Forms of Modernity in African America* (Ann Arbor: University of Michigan Press, 2000), 3.

Notes to Chapter 2

1. Cited in *A Treasury of Afro-American Folklore*, edited by Harold Courlander (New York: Smithmark Publishers, 1976, 1996), 532.

2. Sidney W. Mintz and Richard Price, *The Birth of African American Culture: An Anthropological Perspective* (Boston: Beacon Press, 1976; Preface, 1992), 10.

3. Guerin Montilius, *Dompim: The Spirituality of African Peoples* (Nashville: Winston-Derek Publishers, 1989), 2.

4. Ibid., 3–4.

5. Aylward Shorter, *Prayer in the Religious Traditions of Africa*, (New York: Oxford University Press, 1976), 60.

6. Albert J. Raboteau, "The Afro-American Traditions," in *Caring and Curing: Health and Medicine in the Western Religious Traditions*, edited by Ronald L. Numbers and Darrel W. Amundsen (New York: Macmillan, 1986), 542.

7. Peter J. Paris, *The Spirituality of African Peoples: The Search for a Common Moral Discourse* (Minneapolis: Fortress Press, 1995), 118.

8. Linda Villarosa, editor, *Body and Soul: The Black Women's Guide to Physical Health and Emotional Well-Being* (New York: Harper Perennial, 1994), 5.

9. Ibid.

10. Janis Coombs Epps, "On Cancer and Conjuring," in *The Black Women's Health Book: Speaking for Ourselves*, edited by Evelyn C. White (Seattle: Seal Press, 1990), 38–43.

11. Charles P. Henry, *Culture and African American Politics*, Blacks in the Diaspora Series, edited by Darlene Clark Hine et al. (Bloomington: Indiana University Press, 1990), 107.

12. Will Coleman, *Tribal Talk: Black Theology, Hermeneutics, and African/American Ways of "Telling the Story"* (University Park: Pennsylvania University Press, 2000), 36.

13. Ibid., 65.

14. Elliott P. Skinner, "Hegemonic Paradigms and the African World: Striving to be Free," in *Crossing Boundaries: Comparative History of Black People*, edited by Darlene Clark Hine and Jacqueline McLeod (Bloomington: Indiana University Press, 1999), 45.

15. For example, see Walter Johnson, *Soul by Soul: Life inside the Antebellum Slave Market* (Cambridge: Harvard University Press, 1999), which discusses the processes by which black people were turned into labor products, as well as some ways that black people utilized to resist being defined by enslavement.

16. Ibid., 149.

17. For a more thorough discussion of these concepts, see George W.

Stocking Jr., *Victorian Anthropology* (New York: Free Press, 1987). Note particularly chapter 1, 9–45.

18. Samuel Cartwright, "The Prognathous Species of Mankind," in *Slavery Defended: The Views of the Old South,* edited by Eric L. McKitrick (Englewood Cliffs, NJ: Prentice-Hall, 1963), 143.

19. Thornton Stringfellow, "A Scriptural View of Slavery," in *Slavery Defended: The Views of the Old South,* edited by Eric L. McKitrick (Englewood Cliffs, NJ: Prentice-Hall, 1963), 92 (emphasis mine).

20. David Walker, *Appeal to the Coloured Citizens of the World but in Particular, and Very Expressly, to Those of the United States of America* (New York: Hill and Wang, rev. ed., 1995), 12, 16.

21. Sean Wilentz, Introduction to Walker, *Appeal,* xix.

22. Cartwright, "The Prognathous Species of Mankind," 143.

23. Anna Julia Cooper, *A Voice from the South* (New York: Oxford University Press, 1988), 125.

24. W. E. B. Du Bois, *Dusk of Dawn: An Essay Toward an Autobiography of a Race Concept* (New York: Schocken Books, 1968), 665–66.

25. Robert E. Hood, *Begrimed and Black: Christian Traditions on Blacks and Blackness* (Minneapolis: Fortress Press, 1994), 181.

26. Sarah Chinn, *Technology and the Logic of American Racism: A Cultural History of the Body as Evidence* (London: Continuum, 2000), 18.

27. Ibid., 19.

28. Marcellus Andrews, *The Political Economy of Hope and Fear: Capitalism and the Black Condition in America* (New York: New York University Press, 1990).

29. An offhand comment by the white social commentator William Bennett about black abortion as a way to control crime created a furor. Bennett and his supporters defended the statement because it was made as a way to describe the horrors of abortion. However, many other Americans were grossly offended that Bennett would automatically view crime as a *black* issue.

30. Toni Morrison, "Home," in *The House That Race Built,* edited by Wahneema Lubiano (New York: Pantheon Books, 1997), 3.

31. Howard F. Stein, *American Medicine as Culture* (Boulder, CO: Westview Press, 1990), 13.

32. Ibid., 38.

33. Ibid., 35.

34. Susan Smith, *Sick and Tired of Being Sick and Tired: Black Women's Health Activism in America, 1890–1950* (Philadelphia: University of Pennsylvania Press, 1995), 93.

35. The book is James Jones, *Bad Blood: The Tuskegee Syphilis Experiment;* the movie, *Miss Evers' Boys.*

36. Evelyn M. Hammonds, "Your Silence Will Not Protect You: Nurse Eunice Rivers and the Tuskegee Syphilis Study," in *The Black Women's Health Book: Speaking For Ourselves*, edited by Evelyn C. White (Seattle: Seal Press, 1990), 328.

37. Smith, *Sick and Tired of Being Sick and Tired*, 111.

38. Ibid., 115.

39. Hammonds, "Your Silence Will Not Protect You," 325.

40. Bruce Jackson, "The Other Kind of Doctor: Conjure and Magic in Black American Folk Medicine," in *American Folk Medicine*, edited by Wayland D. Hand (Berkeley: University of California Press, 1976), 270.

41. Ibid., 267.

42. Bruno Gebhard, "The Interrelationship of Scientific and Folk Medicine in the United States of America since 1850," in *American Folk Medicine*, edited by Wayland D. Hand (Berkeley: University of California Press, 1976), 94.

43. Ibid., 97.

44. P Jazz interview by author, 8 May 1997, Detroit.

Notes to Chapter 3

1. Stewart E. Tolnay, *The Bottom Rung: African American Family Life on Southern Farms* (Urbana: University of Illinois Press, 1999), 21–23.

2. Thomas J. Sugrue, *The Origins of the Urban Crisis: Race and Inequality in Postwar Detroit* (Princeton: Princeton University Press, 1996), 22–23.

3. Advertisement in monograph by James Samuel Stemons, "The North Holds the Key to the Race Question" (Philadelphia: Sumner Press, 1907), back page.

4. William L. Bulkley, "Race Prejudice as Viewed from an Economic Standpoint," in *The Voice of Black America: Major Speeches by Negroes in the U.S., 1797–1971*, edited by Philip S. Foner (New York: Simon and Schuster, 1972), 680.

5. Ms. Essie, interviewed in Detroit, March 2003.

6. Ibid.

7. Joseph Zias, collector, March 14, 1971, Wayne State University Folklore Archives Collection, accession 1729, Box 2, 94.

8. Ibid., 88.

9. Sandra Tamar West, collector, November 20, 1970, Wayne State University Folklore Archives Collection, tape 710, #4114.

10. Ibid.

11. Zias, collector, 158–59.

12. Gloria Lamar Evans, collector, Wayne State University Folklore Archives Collection, 1970, #167, Box 2, collection sheets, 21–57.

13. Gloria Lamar Evans, collector, December 9, 1970, Wayne State University Folklore Archives Collection, tape 707, #4113.

14. Ibid., collection sheets, 3.

15. Zias, collector, 206.

16. Evans, collector, 1970, collection sheets, 21–57.

17. West, collector, tape 710.

18. Zias, collector, 185.

19. Ibid., 81.

20. Ibid., 89.

21. Ibid., 206.

22. Wayne State University Folklore Archives Collection, accession 1729, Box 2, 227.

23. West, collector, November 20, 1970, Wayne State University Folklore Archives Collection, tape 710, #4114.

24. Evans, collector, tape 707.

25. Ibid.

26. Ibid.

27. West, collector, tape 710.

28. Ibid., 85.

29. Ibid., 90–91.

30. Zias, collector, 86.

31. Ibid., 206–7.

32. Listing of these cures is from Gloria Evans, collection sheets, 21–57.

33. Zias, collector, 91, 93.

34. Ibid., 185–86.

35. Dorothy Roberts, *Killing the Black Body: Race, Reproduction and the Meaning of Liberty* (New York: Vintage Books, 1999), 90.

36. Evans, collector, tape 707, #4113.

37. Zias, collector, 86.

38. Ibid., 89.

39. Ibid., 84.

40. Zora Neale Hurston, *I Love Myself When I Am Laughing: A Zora Neale Hurston Reader*, edited by Alice Walker (New York: Feminist Press, 1979), 169.

41. John Langston Gwaltney, *Drylongso: A Self-Portrait of Black America* (New York: New Press, 1993), xxvi.

42. See, for example, Homi K. Bhabha, *The Location of Culture* (London: Routledge, 1994), 112–13.

43. Robert J. C. Young, *Colonial Desire: Hybridity in Theory, Culture and Race* (London: Routledge, 1995), 5.

44. Zias, collector, 133.

45. Carolyn Morrow Long, *Spiritual Merchants: Religion, Magic, and Commerce* (Knoxville: University of Tennessee Press, 2001), 99–100.

46. Loudell Snow, *Walkin' Over Medicine* (Boulder, CO: Westview Press, 1993), 35.

47. William L. Bulkley, "Race Prejudice as Viewed from an Economic Standpoint," in *The Voice of Black America: Major Speeches by Negroes in the U.S., 1797–1971,* edited by Philip S. Foner (New York: Simon and Schuster, 1972), 680.

48. Evelyn Brooks Higginbotham, "Rethinking Vernacular Culture: Black Religion and Race Records in the 1920s and 1930s," in *The House That Race Built: Black Americans, U.S. Terrain,* edited by Wahneema Lubiano (New York: Pantheon Books, 1997), 163.

49. Ibid., 165.

50. Loudell F. Snow, "Traditional Health Beliefs and Practices among Lower Class Black Americans," *Western Journal of Medicine,* December 1983, vol. 139, no. 6, 820–28.

Notes to Chapter 4

1. Melissa Victoria Harris-Lacewell, *Barbershops, Bibles, and BET: Everyday Thought and Black Political Thought* (Princeton: Princeton University Press, 2004), 4.

2. Fayth M. Parks, "When Mighty Waters Rise: African American Folk Healing and the Bible" in *African Americans and the Bible: Sacred Texts and Social Textures,* edited by Vincent L. Wimbush (New York: Continuum, 2001), 662.

3. Ibid.

4. Unnamed informant, recorded by Louise Oliphant, Federal Writers' Project, Augusta, Georgia, 1936–40. #100149, Library of Congress, Manuscripts Division, Washington, D.C.

5. Dwight N. Hopkins, *Being Human: Race, Culture, and Religion* (Minneapolis: Fortress Press, 2005), 169.

6. Ibid., 175.

7. Yvonne P. Chireau, *Religion and the African Conjuring Tradition* (Berkeley: University of California Press, 2003), 151.

8. Laura C. Jarmon, *Wishbone: Reference and Interpretation in Black Folk Literature* (Knoxville: University of Tennessee Press, 2003), 120.

9. Parks, "When Mighty Waters Rise."

10. Zias, collector, 87.

11. John L. Jackson Jr., *Real Black: Adventures in Racial Sincerity* (Chicago: University of Chicago Press, 2005), 18.

12. Tommie Shelby, *We Who Are Dark: The Philosophical Foundations of Black Solidarity* (Cambridge: Harvard University Press, 2005), 224.

13. Ibid., 242.

Notes to Chapter 5

1. Ralph Ellison, *Shadow and Act* (New York: Vintage Books, 1995), 257 (emphasis mine).

2. Flora Wilson Bridges, *Resurrection Song: African-American Spirituality* (Maryknoll, NY: Orbis Books, 2001), 170.

3. Zora Neale Hurston, *The Sanctified Church* (Berkeley, CA: Turtle Island Press, 1981), 70, 71–80.

4. Countee Cullen, "Heritage," reprinted in *The Norton Anthology of African American Literature*, edited by Henry Louis Gates Jr. and Nellie Y. McKay (New York: W. W. Norton, 2004, second ed.), 1347–48.

5. E. Frances White, "Africa on My Mind: Gender, Counter Discourse, and African American Nationalism," in *Is It Nation Time? Contemporary Essays on Black Power and Black Nationalism*, edited by Eddie S. Glaude Jr. (Chicago: University of Chicago Press, 2002), 131.

6. W. E. B. Du Bois, *The Souls of Black Folk* (New York: Bantam Books, 1989), 3.

7. Ibid., 4.

8. Ibid., 3.

9. Annie Barnes, *Say It Loud: Middle-Class Blacks Talk about Racism and What to Do about It* (Cleveland: Pilgrim Press, 2000), 98.

10. Adolph Reed Jr., "Black Particularity Reconsidered," in *Is It Nation Time? Contemporary Essays on Black Power and Black Nationalism*, edited by Eddie S. Glaude Jr. (Chicago: University of Chicago Press, 2002), 49.

11. Cited in Kay Mills, *This Little Light of Mine: The Life of Fannie Lou Hamer* (New York: Plume Books, 1993), 166.

12. Randall Robinson, *The Debt: What America Owes to Blacks* (New York: Plume Books, 2000), 13.

13. See events and news page at www.ncobra.org.

14. Article 101, Declaration from the World Conference Against Racism, Racial Discrimination, Xenophobia, and Related Intolerance, issued September 8, 2001 (emphasis mine).

15. Ibid., Article 104 (emphasis mine).

16. The work of this commission is the subject of the documentary *Long Night's Journey into Day*, by Frances Reid and Deborah Hoffman (2000).

17. Contact information: Heaven 1 LLC, 116 S. Jefferson Davis Pkwy., New Orleans, LA 70119.

Notes to Chapter 6

1. Barbara A. Holmes, *Joy Unspeakable: Contemplative Practices of the Black Church* (Minneapolis: Fortress Press, 2004), 5–6.

2. Ibid., 7.

3. Laura C. Jarmon, *Wishbone: Reference and Interpretation in Black Folk Literature* (Knoxville: University of Tennessee Press, 2003), 217.

4. See also Will B. Gravely, "The Rise of African Churches in America (1786–1822): Re-examining the Contexts," in *African American Religious Studies: An Interdisciplinary Anthology*, edited by Gayraud S. Wilmore (Durham, NC: Duke University Press, 1992), 301–17.

5. Zora Neale Hurston, *The Sanctified Church* (Berkeley, CA: Turtle Island Press, 1981), 85.

6. Ibid., 91.

7. Ibid., 103.

8. Gayraud S. Wilmore, *Pragmatic Spirituality: The Christian Faith through an Africentric Lens* (New York: New York University Press, 2004), 96.

9. Evelyn Brooks Higginbotham, "Rethinking Vernacular Culture: Black Religion and Race Records in the 1920s and 1930s," in *The House That Race Built: Black Americans, U.S. Terrain*, edited by Wahneema Lubiano (New York: Pantheon Books, 1997), 161.

10. James H. Cone, *Risks of Faith: The Emergence of a Black Theology of Liberation, 1968–1998* (Boston: Beacon Press, 1999), 43.

11. Yvonne P. Chireau, *Religion and the African American Conjuring Tradition* (Berkeley: University of California Press, 2003), 151.

12. Malidoma Patrice Somé, *Of Water and the Spirit: Ritual, Magic, and Initiation in the Life of an African Shaman* (New York: G. P. Putnam's Sons, 1994), 287–88.

13. In one text, Teish explains the different layers of the soul understood in one African tradition: the universal, human, sexual, astral, national, racial, ancestral, historical, and guardian. (*Carnival of the Spirit: Seasonal Celebrations and Rites of Passage* [San Francisco: Harper, 1994], 175–79).

14. Joseph M. Murphy, *Working the Spirit: Ceremonies of the African Diaspora* (Boston: Beacon Press, 1994), 7.

15. Margarite Fernández Olmos and Elizabeth Paravisini-Gebert, *Creole Religion of the Caribbean: An Introduction from Vodou and Santería to Obeah and Espiritismo* (New York: New York University Press, 2003), 9.

16. Kamari Maxine Clarke, *Mapping Yorùbá Networks: Power and Agency in the Making of Transnational Communities* (Durham, NC: Duke University Press, 2004), 12.

17. Ibid., 10–11.

18. Delores S. Williams, "Straight Talk, Plain Talk: Womanist Words about Salvation in a Social Context," in *Embracing the Spirit*, edited by Emilie Townes (Maryknoll, NY: Orbis Books, 1997), 99–100.

19. Gayraud S. Wilmore, *Black Religion and Black Radicalism: An Interpreta-*

tion of the Religious History of Afro-American People (Maryknoll, NY: Orbis Books, eighth printing, 1993), 228–29.

20. C. Eric Lincoln, *The Black Muslims in America* (Queens, NY: Kayode Publications, 1973), 12–25.

21. Ibid., 29.

22. Ibid., 31.

23. Claude F. Jacobs, "Rituals of Healing in African American Spiritual Churches," in *Religion and Healing in America,* edited by Linda L. Barnes and Susan S. Sered (New York: Oxford University Press, 2005), 333.

24. Ibid., 338.

25. Ibid., 339.

26. Betty R. Price, *Through the Fire and Through the Water: My Triumph over Cancer* (Los Angeles: Faith One, 1997), 9.

27. Ibid., 22.

28. From Evangelist Cleopatra's written account.

Notes to Chapter 7

1. Yvonne P. Chireau, *Religion and the African American Conjuring Tradition* (Berkeley: University of California Press, 2003), 4.

2. Ibid., 154–55.

3. The other archetypal figures Hopkins develops are the trickster, the outlaw, and the Christian hero.

4. Tayannah Lee McQuillar, *Rootwork: Using the Folk Magick of Black America for Love, Money, and Success* (New York: Simon and Schuster, 2003), 3 (emphasis mine).

5. Ibid., 3–4.

6. Faith Mitchell, *Hoodoo Medicine: Gullah Herbal Remedies* (Columbia, SC: Summerhouse Press, 1999), 33–34.

7. Eric Bailey, *African American Alternative Medicine: Using Alternative Medicine to Prevent and Control Chronic Diseases,* (Westport, CT: Bergin and Garvey, 2002).

8. Ishmael Reed, "Neo-HooDoo Manifesto: Talkin' Mumbo Jumbo and following the Neo-HooDoo Way," in *African Americans and the Bible: Sacred Texts and Social Textures,* edited by Vincent L. Wimbush (New York: Continuum, 2001), 670.

9. Stephanie Rose Bird, *Sticks, Stones, Roots and Bones: Hoodoo, Mojo, and Conjuring with Herbs* (St. Paul, MN: Llewellyn Publications, 2004), 2.

10. Ibid., 26.

11. Ibid., 25.

12. Ibid., 5.

13. Catherine Yronwode, *Hoodoo Herb and Root Magic: A Materia Magica of African-American Conjure* (Forestville, CA: Luck Mojo Curio Company, 2002), 17.

14. Ibid., 13.

15. Carolyn Morrow Long, *Spiritual Merchants: Religion, Magic, and Commerce* (Knoxville: University of Tennessee Press, 2001), 161.

16. Luisha Teish, *Jambalaya: The Natural Woman's Book of Personal Charms and Practical Rituals* (New York: HarperCollins, 1985), 148.

17. Long, *Spiritual Merchants*, 250.

18. www.grandmarosa.com.

19. http://www.luckymojo.com/hoodoohisotry.html.

20. http://www.luckymojo.com/curriculum.html.

21. http://www.mamiwata.com/hoodoo%20interview.html.

22. Onnie Lee Logan, *Motherwit: An Alabama Midwife's Story* (New York: Plume Books, 1991), 89.

23. From a flyer distributed by Renee in class.

24. Bird, *Sticks, Stones, Roots and Bones*, 236–38.

25. Ibid., 246.

Bibliography

Andrews, Marcellus. *The Political Economy of Hope and Fear: Capitalism and the Black Condition in America.* New York: New York University Press, 1990.

Bailey, Eric. *African American Alternative Medicine: Using Alternative Medicine to Prevent and Control Chronic Diseases.* Westport, CT: Bergin and Garvey, 2002.

Baker, Houston A., Jr. *Modernism and the Harlem Renaissance.* Chicago: University of Chicago Press, 1987.

Barnes, Annie. *Say It Loud: Middle-Class Blacks Talk about Racism and What to Do about It.* Cleveland: Pilgrim Press, 2000.

Bascom, William. "Folklore." In *International Encyclopedia of the Social Sciences* (1968), 196–97. Cited in Bascom, "Folklore and the Africanist." *Journal of American Folklore,* vol. 86, no. 341 (July–September 1973): 253–59.

Bhabha, Homi K. *The Location of Culture.* London: Routledge, 1994.

Bird, Stephanie Rose. *Sticks, Stones, Roots and Bones: Hoodoo, Mojo, and Conjuring with Herbs.* St. Paul, MN: Llewellyn Publications, 2004.

Bridges, Flora Wilson. *Resurrection Song: African-American Spirituality.* Maryknoll, NY: Orbis Books, 2001.

Bulkley, William L. "Race Prejudice as Viewed from an Economic Standpoint." In *The Voice of Black America: Major Speeches by Negroes in the U.S., 1797–1971.* Philip S. Foner, editor. New York: Simon and Schuster, 1972. 680–86.

Butler, Lee H., Jr. "The Unpopular Experience of Popular Culture: Cultural Resistance as Identity Formation." *Journal of Pastoral Theology* (June 2001): 40–52.

Chinn, Sarah. *Technology and the Logic of American Racism: A Cultural History of the Body as Evidence.* London: Continuum, 2000.

Chireau, Yvonne P. *Religion and the African American Conjuring Tradition.* Berkeley: University of California Press, 2003.

Clarke, Kamari Maxine. *Mapping Yorùbá Networks: Power and Agency in the Making of Transnational Communities.* Durham, NC: Duke University Press, 2004.

Coleman, Will. *Tribal Talk: Black Theology, Hermeneutics, and African/American Ways of "Telling the Story."* University Park: Pennsylvania State University Press, 2000.

Collins, Patricia Hill. *Fighting Words: Black Women and the Search for Justice.* Minneapolis: University of Minnesota Press, 1998.

Cone, James H. *Risks of Faith: The Emergence of a Black Theology of Liberation, 1968–1998.* Boston: Beacon Press, 1999.

Cooper, Anna Julia. *A Voice from the South.* New York: Oxford University Press, 1988.

Courlander, Harold, editor. *A Treasury of Afro-American Folklore.* New York: Smithmark Publishers, 1996.

Declaration from the World Conference Against Racism, Racial Discrimination, Xenophobia, and Related Intolerance. Durban, South Africa, September 8, 2001.

Du Bois, W. E. B. *Dusk of Dawn: An Essay Toward an Autobiography of a Race Concept.* New York: Schocken Books, 1968.

———. *The Souls of Black Folk.* New York: Bantam Books, 1989.

Dundes, Alan, editor. *Mother Wit from the Laughing Barrel: Readings in the Interpretation of Afro-American Folklore.* Englewood Cliffs, NJ: Prentice-Hall, 1973.

Ellison, Ralph. *Shadow and Act.* New York: Vintage Books, 1995.

Epps, Janis Coombs. "On Cancer and Conjuring." In *The Black Women's Health Book: Speaking for Ourselves.* Edited by Evelyn C. White. Seattle: Seal Press, 1990. 38–43.

Fauset, Arthur Huff. *Black Gods of the Metropolis: Negro Religious Cults of the Urban North.* Vol. 3, Brinton Memorial Series. Philadelphia Anthropological Society, 1944; reprint, University of Pennsylvania Press, 1971.

Gates, Henry Louis, Jr., and Nellie Y. McKay, editors. *Norton Anthology of African American Literature.* New York: W. W. Norton, 2004.

Gebhard, Bruno. "The Interrelationship of Scientific and Folk Medicine in the United States of America since 1850." In *American Folk Medicine.* Edited by Wayland D. Hand. Berkeley: University of California Press, 1976. 91–98.

Genovese, Eugene D. *Roll Jordan Roll: The World the Slaves Made.* New York: Vintage Books, 1976.

Goodson, Martia Graham. "Medical-Botanical Contributions of African Slave Women to American Medicine." In *Black Women in American History.* Edited by Darlene Clark Hine. New York: Carlson Publishing, 1990. 1–10.

Gravely, Will B. "The Rise of African Churches in America (1786–1822): Reexamining the Contexts." In *African American Religious Studies: An Interdisciplinary Anthology.* Edited by Gayraud S. Wilmore. Durham, NC: Duke University Press, 1992. 301–17.

Gwaltney, John Langston. *Drylongso: A Self-Portrait of Black America.* New York: New Press, 1993.

Hammonds, Evelyn M. "Your Silence Will Not Protect You: Nurse Eunice Rivers and the Tuskegee Syphilis Study." In *The Black Women's Health*

Book: Speaking for Ourselves. Edited by Evelyn C. White. Seattle: Seal Press, 1990. 323–31.

Harris-Lacewell, Melissa Victoria. *Barbershops, Bibles, and BET: Everyday Thought and Black Political Thought.* Princeton: Princeton University Press, 2004.

Henry, Charles P. *Culture and African American Politics.* Blacks in the Diaspora Series. Edited by Darlene Clark Hine. Bloomington: Indiana University Press, 1990.

Higginbotham, Evelyn Brooks. "Rethinking Vernacular Culture: Black Religion and Race Records in the 1920s and 1930s." In *The House That Race Built: Black Americans, U.S. Terrain.* Edited by Wahneema Lubiano. New York: Pantheon Books, 1997. 157–77.

Hirsch, E. D., Jr. *Cultural Literacy: What Every American Needs to Know.* New York: Vintage Books, 1988.

Holmes, Barbara A. *Joy Unspeakable: Contemplative Practices of the Black Church.* Minneapolis: Fortress Press, 2004.

Holmes, David G. *Revisiting Racialized Voice: African American Ethos in Language and Literature.* Carbondale: Southern Illinois University Press, 2004.

Hood, Robert E. *Begrimed and Black: Christian Traditions on Blacks and Blackness.* Minneapolis: Fortress Press, 1994.

Hopkins, Dwight N. *Being Human: Race, Culture, and Religion.* Minneapolis: Fortress Press, 2005.

Hurston, Zora Neale. *Go Gator and Muddy the Waters: Writings by Zora Neale Hurston from the Federal Writers' Project.* New York: W. W. Norton, 1999.

———. *I Love Myself When I Am Laughing: A Zora Neale Hurston Reader.* Edited by Alice Walker. New York: Feminist Press, 1979.

———. *The Sanctified Church.* Berkeley, CA: Turtle Island Press, 1981.

Jackson, Bruce. "The Other Kind of Doctor: Conjure and Magic in Black American Folk Medicine." In *American Folk Medicine.* Edited by Wayland D. Hand. Berkeley: University of California Press, 1976. 259–72.

Jackson, John L., Jr. *Real Black: Adventures in Racial Sincerity.* Chicago: University of Chicago Press, 2005.

Jacobs, Claude F. "Rituals of Healing in African American Spiritual Churches." In *Religion and Healing in America.* Edited by Linda L. Barnes and Susan S. Sered. New York: Oxford University Press, 2005. 333–41.

Jarmon, Laura C. *Wishbone: Reference and Interpretation in Black Folk Literature.* Knoxville: University of Tennessee Press, 2003.

Johnson, Walter. *Soul by Soul: Life Inside the Antebellum Slave Market.* Cambridge: Harvard University Press, 1999.

Levine, Lawrence W. *Black Culture and Black Consciousness: Afro-American Folk Thought from Slavery to Freedom.* New York: Oxford University Press, 1977.

Logan, Onnie Lee. *Motherwit: An Alabama Midwife's Story.* New York: Plume Books, 1991.

Long, Carolyn Morrow. *Spiritual Merchants: Religion, Magic, and Commerce.* Knoxville: University of Tennessee Press, 2001.

McGregory, Jerrilyn M. *"There Are Other Ways to Get Happy": African-American Urban Folklore.* Ann Arbor: University of Michigan Press, 1992.

McKitrick, Eric L., editor. *Slavery Defended: The Views of the Old South.* Englewood Cliffs, NJ: Prentice-Hall, 1963.

McQuillar, Tayannah Lee. *Rootwork: Using the Folk Magick of Black America for Love, Money, and Success.* New York: Simon and Schuster, 2003.

Mills, Kay. *This Little Light of Mine: The Life of Fannie Lou Hamer.* New York: Plume Books, 1993.

Mintz, Sidney W., and Richard Price. *The Birth of African American Culture: An Anthropological Perspective.* Boston: Beacon Press, 1976; Preface, 1992.

Montilius, Guerin. *Dompim: The Spirituality of African Peoples.* Nashville: Winston-Derek Publishers, 1989.

Morrison, Toni. "Home." In *The House that Race Built: Black Americans, U.S. Terrain.* Edited by Wahneema Lubiano. New York: Pantheon Books, 1997. 3–12.

Murphy, Joseph M. *Working the Spirit: Ceremonies of the African Diaspora.* Boston: Beacon Press, 1994.

National Coalition of Blacks for Reparations in America, www.ncobra.org.

Nicholls, David G. *Conjuring the Folk: Forms of Modernity in African America.* Ann Arbor: University of Michigan Press, 2000.

Olmos, Margarite Fernández, and Elizabeth Paravisini-Gebert. *Creole Religions of the Caribbean: An Introduction from Vodou and Santería to Obeah and Espiritismo.* New York: New York University Press, 2003.

Paris, Peter J. *The Spirituality of African Peoples: The Search for a Common Moral Discourse.* Minneapolis: Fortress Press, 1995.

Parks, Fayth M. "When Mighty Waters Rise: African American Folk Healing and the Bible." In *African Americans and the Bible: Sacred Texts and Social Textures.* Edited by Vincent L. Wimbush. New York: Continuum, 2001. 661–70.

Prendergast, Catherine. *Literacy and Racial Justice: The Politics of Learning after Brown v. Board of Education.* Carbondale: Southern Illinois University Press, 2003.

Price, Betty R. *Through the Fire and Through the Water: My Triumph over Cancer.* Los Angeles: Faith One, 1997.

Raboteau, Albert J. "The Afro-American Traditions." In *Caring and Curing: Health and Medicine in the Western Religious Traditions.* Edited by Ronald L. Numbers and Darrel W. Amundsen. New York: Macmillan, 1986. 539–62.

Reed, Adolph, Jr. "Black Particularity Reconsidered." In *Is It Nation Time? Con-*

temporary Essays on Black Power and Black Nationalism. Edited by Eddie S. Glaude Jr. Chicago: University of Chicago Press, 2002. 39–66.

Reed, Ishmael. "Neo-HooDoo Manifesto: Talkin' Mumbo Jumbo and Following the Neo-HooDoo Way." In *African Americans and the Bible: Sacred Texts and Social Textures.* Edited by Vincent L. Wimbush. New York: Continuum, 2001. 670.

Roberts, Dorothy. *Killing the Black Body: Race, Reproduction and the Meaning of Liberty.* New York: Vintage Books, 1999.

Robinson, Randall. *The Debt: What America Owes to Blacks.* New York: Plume, 2000.

Shelby, Tommie. *We Who Are Dark: The Philosophical Foundations of Black Solidarity.* Cambridge: Harvard University Press, 2005.

Shorter, Aylward. *Prayer in the Religious Traditions of Africa.* New York: Oxford University Press, 1976.

Skinner, Elliott P. "Hegemonic Paradigms and the African World: Striving to Be Free." In *Crossing Boundaries: Comparative History of Black People in Diaspora.* Edited by Darlene Clark Hine and Jacqueline McLeod Bloomington: Indiana University Press, 1999. 45–70.

Smith, Susan. *Sick and Tired of Being Sick and Tired: Black Women's Health Activism in America, 1890–1950.* Philadelphia: University of Pennsylvania Press, 1995.

Snow, Loudell F. " 'I Was Born Just Exactly with the Gift': An Interview with a Voodoo Practitioner." *Journal of American Folklore,* vol. 86, no. 341 (July–September 1973): 273–81.

———. "Traditional Health Beliefs and Practices among Lower Class Black Americans." *Western Journal of Medicine,* vol. 139, no. 6 (December 1983): 820–28.

———. *Walkin' Over Medicine.* Boulder, CO: Westview Press, 1993.

Somé, Malidoma Patrice. *Of Water and the Spirit: Ritual, Magic, and Initiation in the Life of an African Shaman.* New York: G. P. Putnam's Sons, 1994.

Stein, Howard F. *American Medicine as Culture.* Boulder, CO: Westview Press, 1990.

Stemons, James Samuel. "The North Holds the Key to the Race Question." Philadelphia: Sumner Press, 1907.

Stocking, George W., Jr. *Victorian Anthropology.* New York: Free Press, 1987.

Stuckey, Sterling. *Slave Culture: Nationalist Theory and the Foundations of Black America.* New York: Oxford University Press, 1987.

Sugrue, Thomas J. *The Origins of the Urban Crisis: Race and Inequality in Postwar Detroit.* Princeton: Princeton University Press, 1996.

Teish, Luisha. *Carnival of the Spirit: Seasonal Celebrations and Rites of Passage.* San Francisco: Harper, 1994.

Teish, Luisha. *Jambalaya: The Natural Woman's Book of Personal Charms and Practical Rituals*. New York: HarperCollins, 1985.

Tolnay, Stewart E. *The Bottom Rung: African American Family Life on Southern Farms*. Urbana: University of Illinois Press, 1999.

Villarosa, Linda, editor. *Body and Soul: The Black Women's Guide to Physical Health and Emotional Well-Being*. New York: HarperPerennial, 1994.

Walker, David. *Appeal to the Coloured Citizens of the World but in Particular, and Very Expressly, to Those of the United States of America*. New York: Hill and Wang, rev. ed., 1995.

Wayne State University Folklore Archives Collection.

White, Deborah Gray. *Ar'n't I a Woman? Female Slaves in the Plantation South*. New York: W. W. Norton, 1985.

White, E. Frances. "Africa on my Mind: Gender, Counter Discourse, and African American Nationalism." In *Is It Nation Time? Contemporary Essays on Black Power and Black Nationalism*. Edited by Eddie S. Glaude Jr. Chicago: University of Chicago Press 2002. 130–55.

Williams, Delores S. "Straight Talk, Plain Talk: Womanist Words about Salvation in a Social Context." In *Embracing the Spirit: Womanist Perspectives on Hope, Salvation and Transformation*. Edited by Emilie M. Townes. Maryknoll, NY: Orbis Books, 1997. 97–121.

Williams, Patricia J. *The Alchemy of Race and Rights: Diary of a Law Professor*. Cambridge: Harvard University Press, 1991.

———. "The Ethnic Scarring of American Whiteness." In *The House That Race Built: Black Americans, U.S. Terrain*. Edited by Wahneema Lubiano. New York: Pantheon Books, 1997. 253–63.

Wilmore, Gayraud S. *Black Religion and Black Radicalism: An Interpretation of the Religious History of Afro-American People*. Maryknoll, NY: Orbis Books, 1993. Eighth printing.

———. *Pragmatic Spirituality: The Christian Faith through an Africentric Lens*. New York: New York University Press, 2004.

Works Progress Administration Slave Narrative Project, Georgia Narratives, Library of Congress, Manuscript Division, http://memory.loc.gov/mss/mesn/044/266262.gif, November 2002.

Works Progress Administration Slave Narrative Project, Georgia Narratives. Louise Oliphant, interviewer, Augusta, Georgia, 1936–1938. Library of Congress, Manuscript Division. http://memory.loc.gov/, November 29, 2002.

Young, Robert J. C. *Colonial Desire: Hybridity in Theory, Culture and Race*. London: Routledge, 1995.

Index

About the Author

Stephanie Y. Mitchem, an associate professor at the University of South Carolina, focuses her research on exploring the rich religious contexts and meanings of African American women and men, while critiquing social injustices structured into American society. She is the author of *Introducing Womanist Theology* (Orbis Books, 2002), *African American Women Tapping Power and Spiritual Wellness* (Pilgrim Press, 2004), and numerous articles.